Musical Quilt Blocks

by Linda Causee

Bobbie Matela	MANAGING EDITOR
Carol Wilson Mansfield	ART DIRECTOR
Linda Causee	EDITORIAL DIRECTOR
Christina Wilson	ASSOCIATE EDITOR
Wendy Mathson	GRAPHIC DESIGNER/ EDITORIAL ASSISTANT

Pictured blocks made by Linda Causee and Christina Wilson

Introduction

When my son joined his high school's marching band in 1995, music became a big part of my life. Now, as my daughter enters her third year as part of the band, I have brought music to my quilting with *Musical Quilt Blocks*.

This musical collection includes two dozen full-size block patterns that can be used for wall hangings, bed quilts, lap quilts, potholders, pillows or wearables. There are plenty of musical notes and instruments–even a jukebox and old-fashioned Victrola!

Don't be intimidated by the small pieces on some of the blocks. Complete foundation piecing instructions, along with full-color patterns, make sewing the blocks easier than ever.

So, put on a favorite CD and listen to the hum of your sewing machine as you construct your favorite musical blocks.

Linda Causee

Thank you to the following companies who generously supplied products for our blocks:

Bernina® of America: Artista 180 sewing machine

Güterman: 100% cotton sewing thread

Springs, Northcott, Bernartex, Moda, FreeSpirit: assorted fabrics

For a full-color catalog including books on quilting, write to:

American School of Needlework® Consumer Division
1455 Linda Vista Drive
San Marcos, CA 92069

e-mail us at: catalog@asnpub.com
visit us at: www.asnpub.com

©2002 by American School of Needlework®, Inc.; ASN Publishing, 1455 Linda Vista Drive, San Marcos, CA 92069

Reprinting or duplicating the information, photographs or graphics in this publication by any means, including copy machine, computer scanning, digital photography, e-mail, personal website and fax, is illegal. Failure to abide by federal copyright laws may result in litigation and fines.

We have made every effort to insure the accuracy and completeness of these instructions. We cannot, however, be responsible for human error, typographical mistakes, or variations in individual work.

ISBN:1-59012-024-8   All rights reserved.   Printed in U. S. A.   123456789

General Directions

About the Patterns
All of the patterns in this book are full size. Several of the blocks have more than one section that must be foundation-pieced individually, then sewn together. Bold lines that are also the cutting lines indicate these sections. A piecing diagram is included with each multi-section block showing the piecing order of the sections.

Also included with each block pattern is a photograph showing the completed block. Note the finished blocks are mirror images of the original patterns, **Fig 1**.

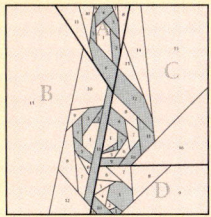 

Pattern   Finished Block (mirror image)

Fig 1

The Foundation Piecing Method
Foundation Material
Before you start sewing, you need to decide the type of foundation on which to piece your blocks. There are several options. Paper is a popular choice for machine piecing because it is readily available and inexpensive. Copier paper, tracing paper or newsprint work well. The paper is removed after the blocks are completely sewn.

Another alternative for foundation piecing is muslin or cotton fabric that is light-colored and lightweight for easy tracing. The fabric will add another layer that you will have to quilt through, but that is only a consideration if you are going to hand quilt. Also, if you use a fabric foundation, you will be able to hand piece your blocks if that is your desire.

A third option for foundation material is Tear Away® or Fun-dation™ translucent non-woven material. Like muslin, it is light enough to see through for tracing, but like paper, it can later be easily removed before quilting.

A new type of "disappearing" foundation material by W.H. Collins is called WashAway™ foundation paper. After sewing, place block in water and the foundation dissolves in 10 seconds.

Preparing the Foundation
Tracing the Block
Trace the block pattern carefully onto your chosen foundation material. Use a ruler and a fine-point permanent marker or fine-line mechanical pencil to make straight lines; be sure to include all numbers and letters for multiple sections.

Cut 1/4" outside of the outer drawn line. Repeat for the number of blocks needed for your quilt.

Transferring the Block
The block pattern can also be transferred onto foundation material, but to do this involves an additional step if you want your block to look like the photographed block. First, trace the block pattern onto tracing paper. Flop the paper so that the design is "backwards" and trace again onto plain paper using a transfer pen or pencil, **Fig 2**.

 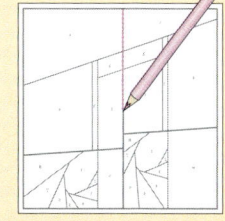

Trace.   Flop and trace again.

Fig 2

Then, following manufacturers' directions, iron transferred design onto foundation material. If these steps are not followed, your finished block will be a mirror image of the finished block shown, **Fig 3**.

Finished Block   Mirror Image

Fig 3

Fabric
We recommend using 100% cotton fabric for piecing. By using cotton rather than cotton/polyester blends, the pieces will not slip as easily and they will respond better to finger pressing.

Pre-washing fabric is not necessary, but it is advisable to test your fabric to make certain that the fabric is colorfast (don't trust manufacturers' labels). Place a 2"-wide strip (cut crosswise) of fabric into a bowl of extremely hot water; if the water changes color, the fabric is bleeding and it will be necessary to wash that fabric until all of the excess dye has washed out. Repeat for all fabrics that will be used for your quilt. Fabrics that continue to bleed after they have been washed several times should be eliminated.

To test for shrinkage, take each saturated strip (used above in the colorfast test) and iron it dry with a hot iron. When the strip is completely dry, measure and compare it to your original 2" measurements. If all of your strips shrink about the same amount, then you really have no problem. When you wash your quilt, you may achieve the puckered look of an antique quilt. If you do not want this look, you will have to wash and dry all fabric before beginning so that shrinkage is no longer an issue. If any of your test strips are shrinking more than the others, these fabrics will need to be pre-washed and dried, or discarded.

Cutting the Fabric

One of biggest advantages to foundation piecing is that you do not have to cut exact pieces for every block. This is especially important for smaller blocks or blocks with many small pieces. It is much easier to handle a small section or strip of fabric than it is to handle a triangle where the finished size of the sides is 1/4".

The main consideration for using fabric pieces for a particular space is that the fabric must be at least 1/4" larger on all sides than the space it is to cover. Squares and strips are easy to figure, but triangle shapes can be a little tricky to piece. Use generous-sized fabric pieces and be careful when positioning the pieces onto the foundation. You do waste some fabric this way, but the time it saves in cutting will be worth it in the end.

Hint: Many of the blocks contain irregularly-shaped triangles. Measure the widest point of the triangle and cut a strip of fabric 1/2" to 1" wider for piecing, **Fig 4**.

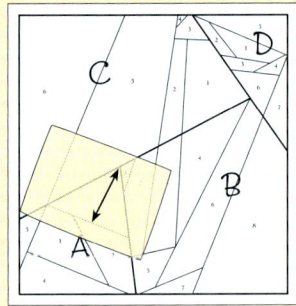

Fig 4

How to Make a Foundation-Pieced Block

1. Prepare foundations as described on the previous page in *Preparing the Foundation*. Cut foundation apart along the bold lines to separate pattern into sections, **Fig 5**.

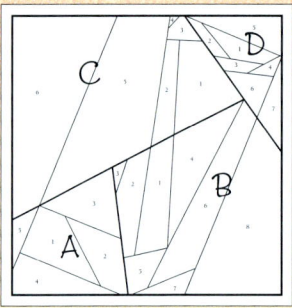

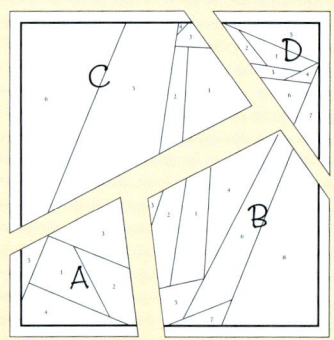

Fig 5

2. Turn foundation section with unmarked side facing you and position piece 1 right side up over the space marked "1" on the foundation. Hold foundation up to a light source to make sure that fabric overlaps at least 1/4" on all sides of space 1. Pin or use a glue stick to hold fabric in place, **Fig 6**.

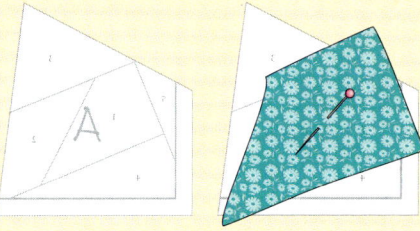

Fig 6

Hint: Use only a small dab of a glue stick to hold fabric in place.

3. Turn foundation over. With marked side of foundation facing you, fold foundation forward along line between space 1 and 2 and trim fabric about 1/8" to 1/4" from fold, **Fig 7**.

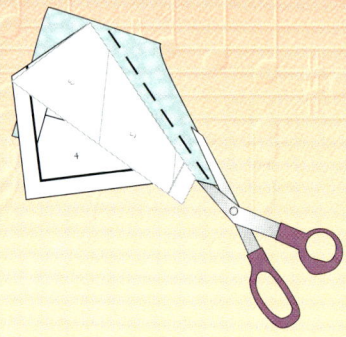

Fig 7

4. Place fabric piece 2 right sides together with piece 1; edge of fabric 2 should be even with just-trimmed edge of fabric 1, **Fig 8**.

Fig 8

Double check to see if fabric piece chosen will cover space 2 completely by folding over along line between space 1 and 2, **Fig 9**.

Fig 9

5. With marked side of foundation facing you, place on sewing machine, holding fabric pieces

together. Sew along line between spaces 1 and 2 using a very small stitch (18 to 20 stitches per inch), **Fig 10**. Begin and end sewing two to three stitches beyond line. You do not need to backstitch.

Fig 10

Hint: Sewing with a very tiny stitch will allow for easier paper removal later. If paper falls apart after stitching, your stitch length is too small and you will need to lengthen the stitch slightly.

6. Turn foundation over. Open piece 2 and finger-press seam, **Fig 11**. Use a pin or dab of glue stick to hold piece in place if necessary.

Fig 11

7. Turn foundation with marked side of foundation facing you; fold foundation forward along line between spaces 1, 2 and 3 and trim about $1/8$" to $1/4$" from fold, **Fig 12**.

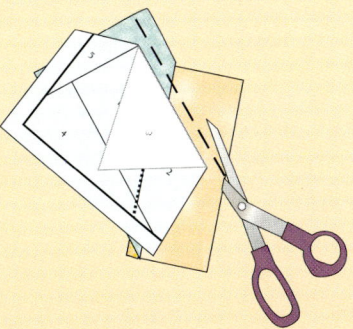

Fig 12

Hint: If using a paper foundation, carefully pull paper away from stitching for easier trimming. If using a fabric foundation, fold it forward as far as it will go and trim.

8. Place fabric 3 right side down, even with just-trimmed edge, **Fig 13**.

Fig 13

9. Turn foundation to marked side and sew along line between spaces 1, 2 and 3; begin and end sewing two to three stitches beyond line, **Fig 14**.

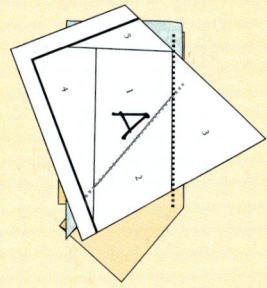

Fig 14

10. Turn foundation over, open piece 3 and finger-press seam. Glue or pin in place, **Fig 15**.

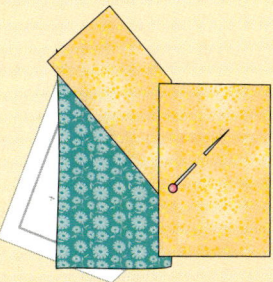

Fig 15

11. Turn foundation with marked side facing you. Fold foundation forward along line between spaces 1, 2 and 4; trim to about $1/8$" to $1/4$" from fold, **Fig 16**.

Fig 16

12. Place fabric 4 right side down, even with just-trimmed edge. With marked side of foundation facing you, sew along line between spaces 1, 2 and 4, **Fig 17**.

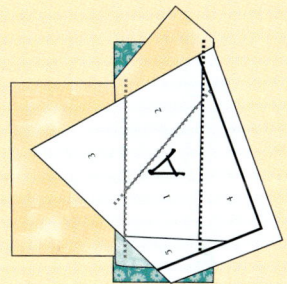

Fig 17

13. Continue trimming and sewing pieces in numerical order until section is complete, **Fig 18**. Make sure pieces along the outer edge are large enough to allow for the $1/4$" seam allowance.

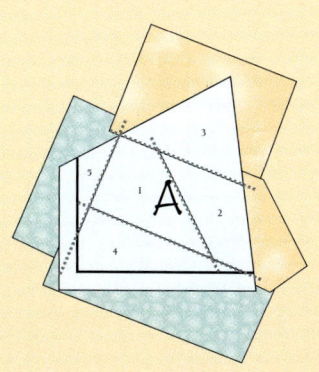

Fig 18

14. Press, then trim fabric 1/4" from outside line of foundation to complete section, **Fig 19**.

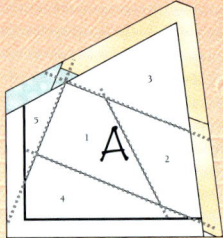

Fig 19

15. Complete remaining sections of block in same manner, **Fig 20**.

Fig 20

Hint: Do not remove paper yet. It is better to remove paper after blocks have been sewn together. Since grain line wasn't considered in piecing, outer edges may be on the bias and, therefore, stretchy. Keeping paper in place until after sewing will prevent the blocks from becoming distorted. Staystitching along outer edge of block, **Fig 21**, *will also help keep fabric from stretching out of shape.*

Fig 21

16. To sew sections together, place right sides together; push a pin through corner of top section going through to corner of bottom section.

Check to be sure pin goes through both corners and is perpendicular (going straight up) to section. If not, pin again until corners match. Repeat at opposite corner to match seams, **Fig 22**.

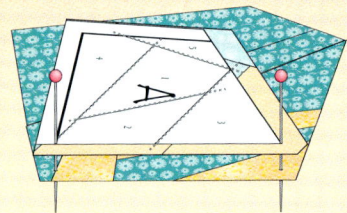

Fig 22

Once pieces are lined up correctly, sew along edge of foundation using a regular stitch length, **Fig 23**.

Fig 23

Hint: If desired, baste sections together by hand or machine. Check sections again; if everything matches up, sew together with regular stitches. Basting takes a little time, but the extra effort will be worth it in the end.

Highlights and Hints for Foundation Piecing

- Begin and end sewing at least two to three stitches beyond line you are sewing on, **Fig 24**.

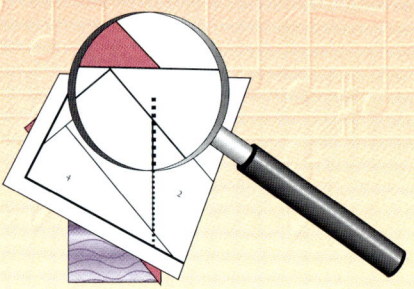

Fig 24

- Some of the blocks have very tiny pieces, so don't worry if your stitching goes through a whole space and into another space, **Fig 25**; it will not interfere with adding subsequent pieces.

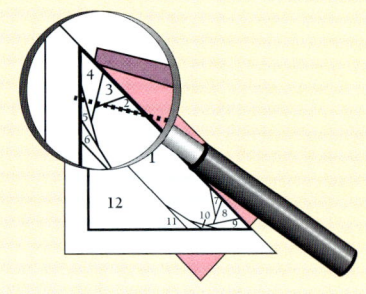

Fig 25

- Finger press or press with an iron after every seam. The little wooden "irons" found in quilt shops or catalogs work great.
- Use a short stitch, around 20 stitches per inch.
- Trim seam allowances to 1/8" to 1/4" (or smaller if necessary).
- Don't worry too much about grainline. Sewing to a foundation stabilizes the fabric and will prevent it from getting out of shape.

- When sewing spaces with points, it is easier to start sewing from the wide end towards the point, **Fig 26**.

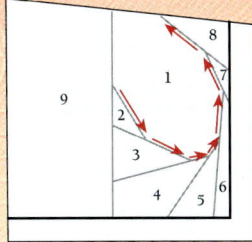

Fig 26

- Directional prints are not recommended unless they are used only once in a block or placed where they can be used easily in a consistent manner, **Fig 27**.

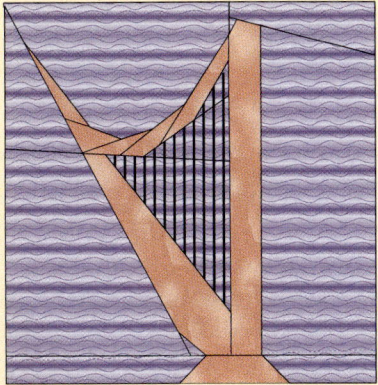

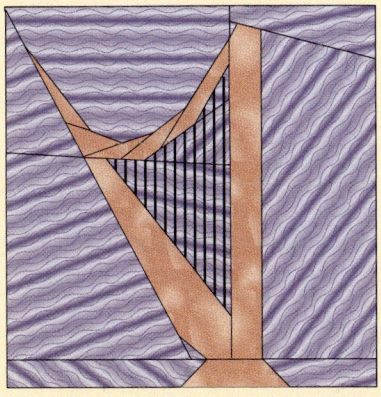

Fig 27

Basic Embroidery Stitches

The following embroidery stitches are used to add details to some of the pieced blocks.

Backstitch

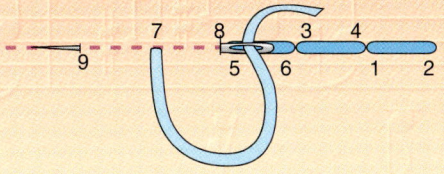

Bring thread up at 1, a stitch length from beginning of design line. Stitch down at 2, at beginning of line. Come up at 3, stitch back down at 4 (same hole as 1). Continue in this manner, stitching backward on the surface to meet the previous stitch. Backstitch can be worked straight or along a curve.

Couching

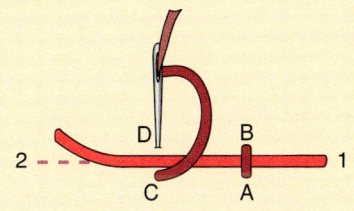

Bring thread up at 1, the beginning of the design line, and position the thread along the marked line. Thread a second needle with a matching or contrasting thread. Stitch up at A, down at B, up at C, etc., taking small stitches to hold or "couch" original thread in place. Stitch down at 2 (end of design line) to end couched thread.

Straight Stitch

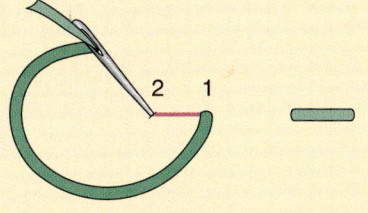

Bring thread up at 1 and down at 2 to cover design line.

Finishing Your Quilt

Making the Quilt Top

Lay out blocks in desired arrangement. Sew quilt blocks together in rows; press seams for rows in alternate directions. Sew rows together, matching seams. Remove all paper foundations.

To add borders, measure quilt top lengthwise; cut two border strips to that length and sew to sides of quilt. Measure quilt top crosswise, including borders just added; cut two border strips to that length. Sew to top and bottom edges of quilt top. Repeat for any additional borders.

Layering the Quilt

There are many types of batting on the market. Use batting that is suitable for the use of your quilt. If making a wallhanging, choose a thin cotton or polyester batting. If making a bed quilt, you may want a low-loft polyester batting for a little more thickness. Check the label to see the quilting requirements and follow those guidelines.

Use 100% cotton fabric for the backing of your quilt. For quilts wider than the 40"- to 44"-wide fabric, you will have to piece your backing unless you use the 90"- to 106"- wide fabrics that are currently available.

Cut backing and batting about 1" to 2" larger on all sides than the quilt top. Place backing wrong side up, then smooth out batting on top. Center quilt top right side up on batting.

Baste layers together using one of the following techniques:

Fusible Iron-on Batting – The new Fusible Batting™ by June Tailor and Gold-Fuse by Mountain Mist® are a wonderful new way to hold the quilt layers together without using other time-consuming methods of basting.

Thread basting – Baste with long stitches, starting in center and sewing toward edges in a number of diagonal lines.

Safety pin basting – Pin through all layers at once, starting from center and working toward edges. Place pins no more than 4" apart, thinking of your quilt plan as you work to make certain pins avoid prospective quilting lines.

Quilt gun basting – Use the handy trigger tool (found in quilt and fabric stores) that pushes nylon tags through all layers of the quilt. Start in center and work randomly toward outside edges. Place tags about 4" apart. You can sew right over the tags and then easily remove them by cutting off with a pair of scissors.

Spray or heat set basting – Use one of the spray adhesives currently on the market, following manufacturer's directions.

Quilting

If you have never used a sewing machine for quilting, you might want to read more about the technique. *Learn to Machine Quilt in Just One Weekend* (ASN #4186), by Marti Michell, is an excellent introduction to machine quilting. This book is available at your local quilt or fabric store, or write the publisher for a list of sources.

You do not need a special machine for quilting. Just make sure your machine is oiled and in good working condition. An even-feed foot is a good investment if you are going to machine quilt, since it is designed to feed the top and bottom layers of the quilt through the machine evenly. Use fine transparent nylon thread in the top and regular sewing thread in the bobbin.

To **quilt in-the-ditch** of a seam (this is actually stitching in the space between two pieces of fabric that have been sewn together), use your fingers to pull blocks or pieces apart slightly and machine stitch right between the two pieces. Try to keep stitching to the side of the seam that does not have the bulk of the seam allowance under it. When you have finished stitching, the quilting will be practically hidden in the seam.

Free form machine quilting is done with a darning foot and the feed dogs down on your sewing machine. It can be used to quilt around a design or to quilt a motif. Free form machine quilting takes practice to master because you are controlling the movement of the quilt under the needle, rather than the machine moving the quilt. With free form machine quilting, you can quilt in any direction: up and down, side to side and even in circles, without pivoting the quilt around the needle.

Attaching the Binding

Trim backing and batting even with quilt top. Cut enough 2½"-wide strips to go around all four sides of quilt, plus 6". Join strips end-to-end with diagonal seams; trim corners, **Fig 28**.

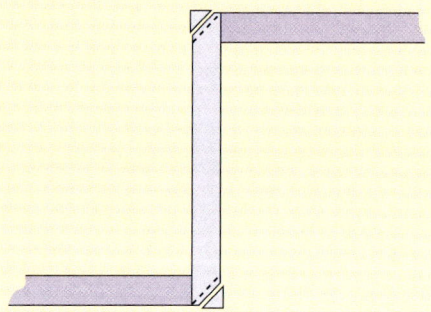

Fig 28

Press seams open. Cut one end of strip at a 45° angle, then press under ¼", **Fig 29**.

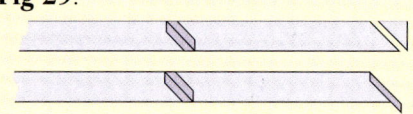

Fig 29

Press entire strip in half lengthwise, wrong sides together, **Fig 30**.

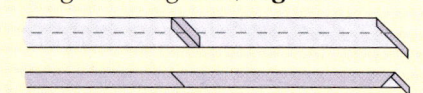

Fig 30

On right side of quilt, position binding in middle of one side, aligning raw edges. Sew binding to quilt using ¼" seam, beginning about an inch below folded end of binding, **Fig 31**.

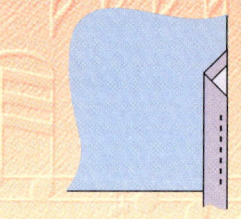

Fig 31

At corner, stop ¼" from edge of quilt and backstitch. Fold binding away from quilt at a 45° angle. Fold binding back on itself so fold is on quilt edge and raw edges are aligned with adjacent side of quilt, **Fig 32**. Begin sewing at quilt edge.

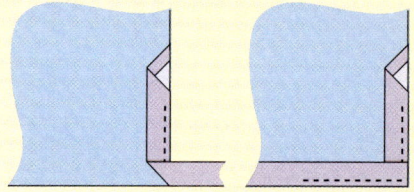

Fig 32

Continue in the same manner around remaining sides of quilt. To finish, stop about two inches away from starting point. Trim excess binding, then tuck inside folded end, **Fig 33**. Finish line of stitching.

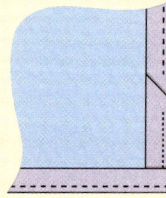

Fig 33

Fold binding to back of quilt so seamline is covered; blindstitch in place.

The Finishing Touch

After your quilt is finished, always sign and date it. A label can be cross stitched, embroidered or even written with a permanent marking pen. To make decorative labels in a hurry, *Iron-on Transfers for Quilt Labels* (ASN #4188) and *Foundation-Pieced Quilt Labels* (ASN #4196), provide many patterns for fun and unique quilt labels. Hand stitch to back of quilt.

#1 French Horn

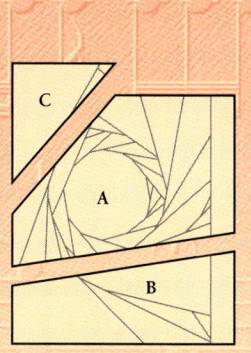
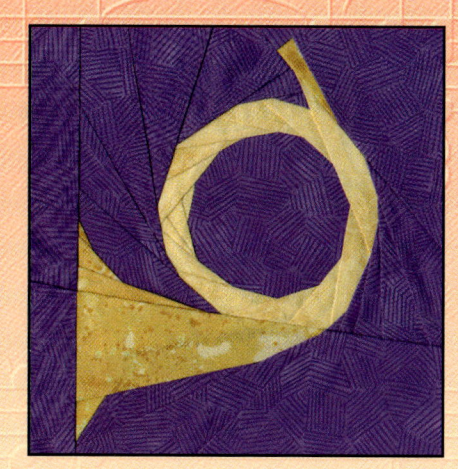

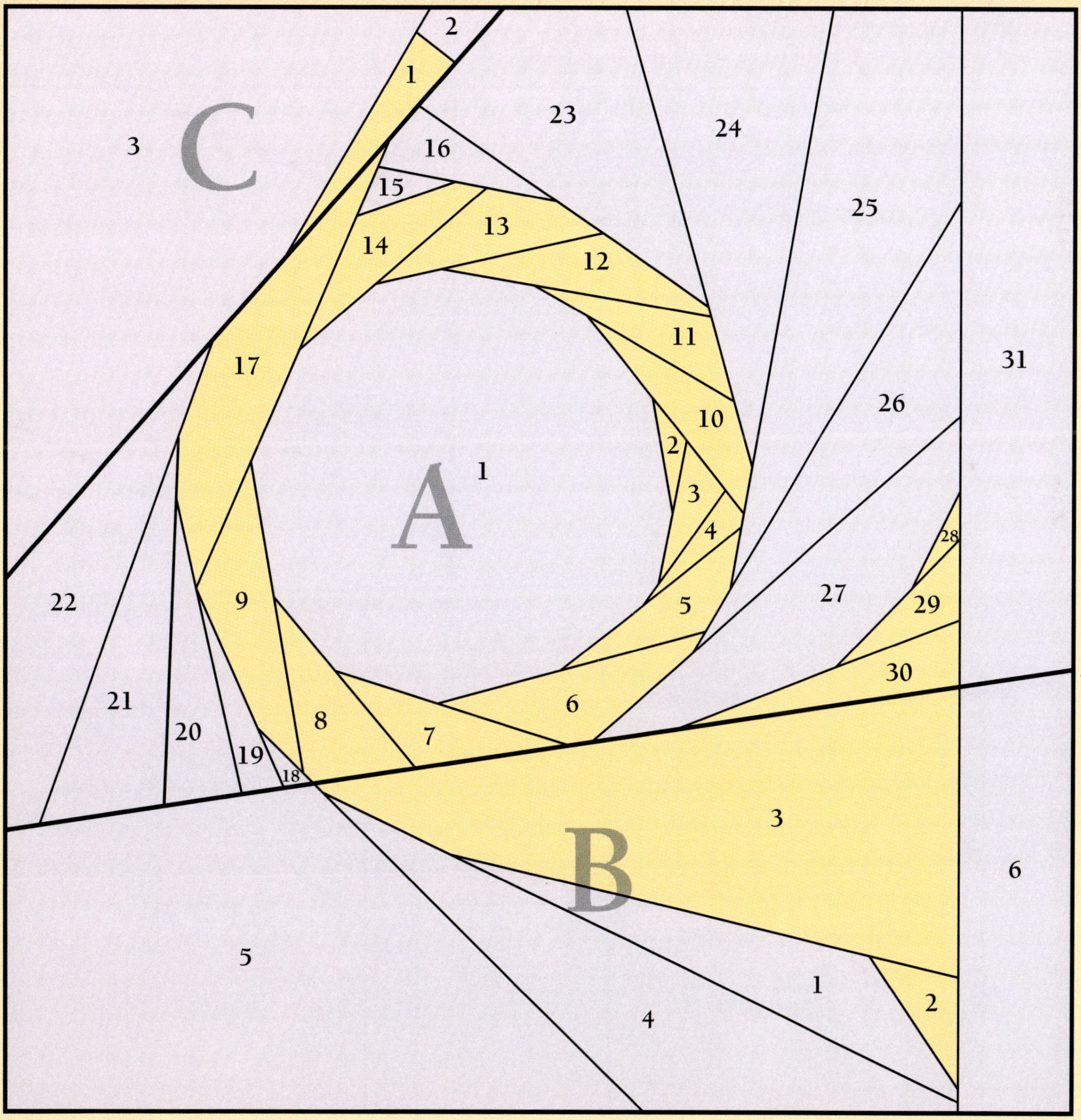

#2 Grand Piano

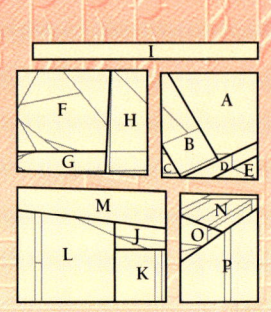

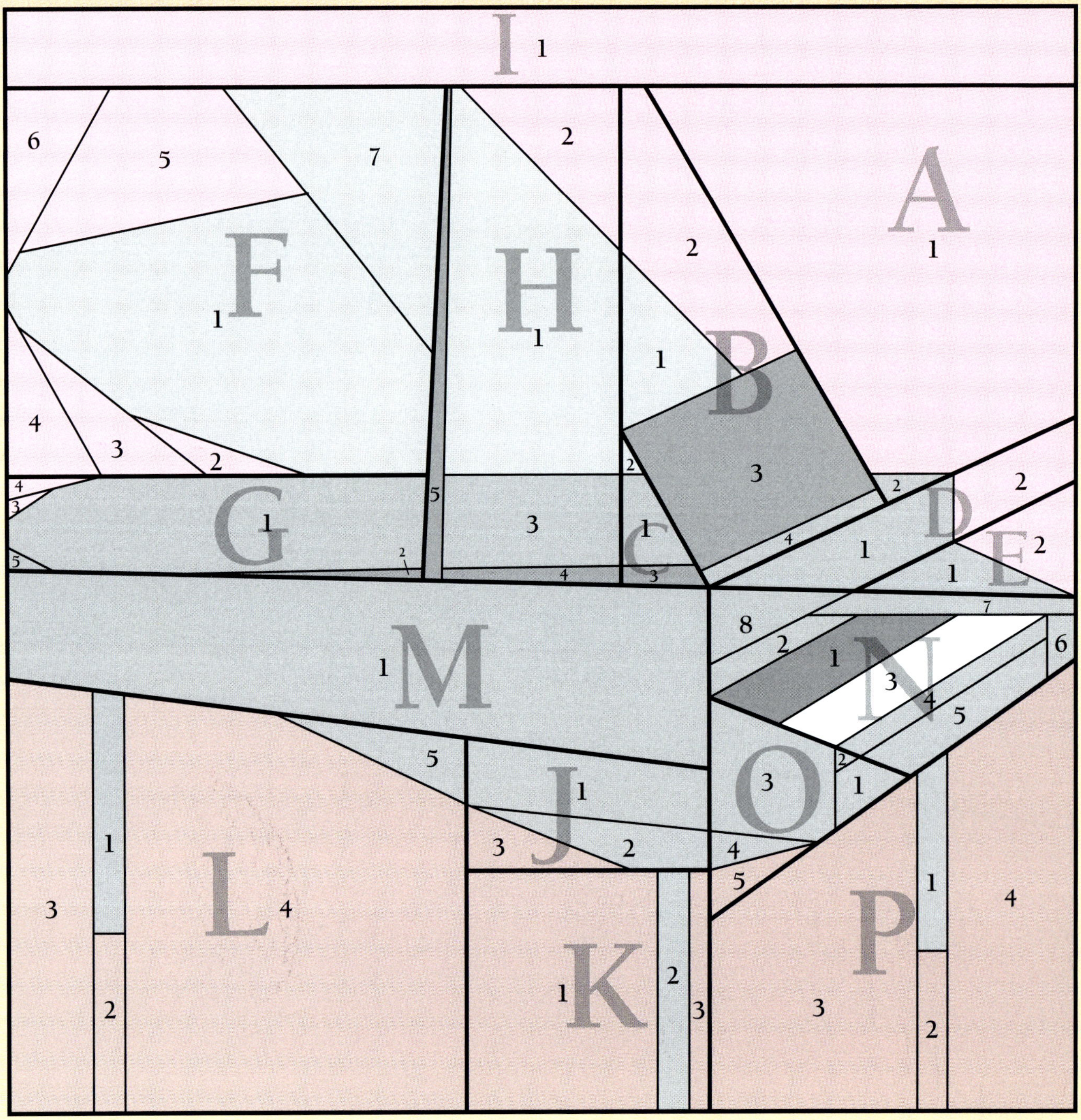

#3 Keyboard

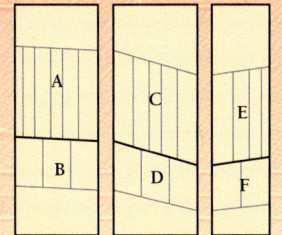

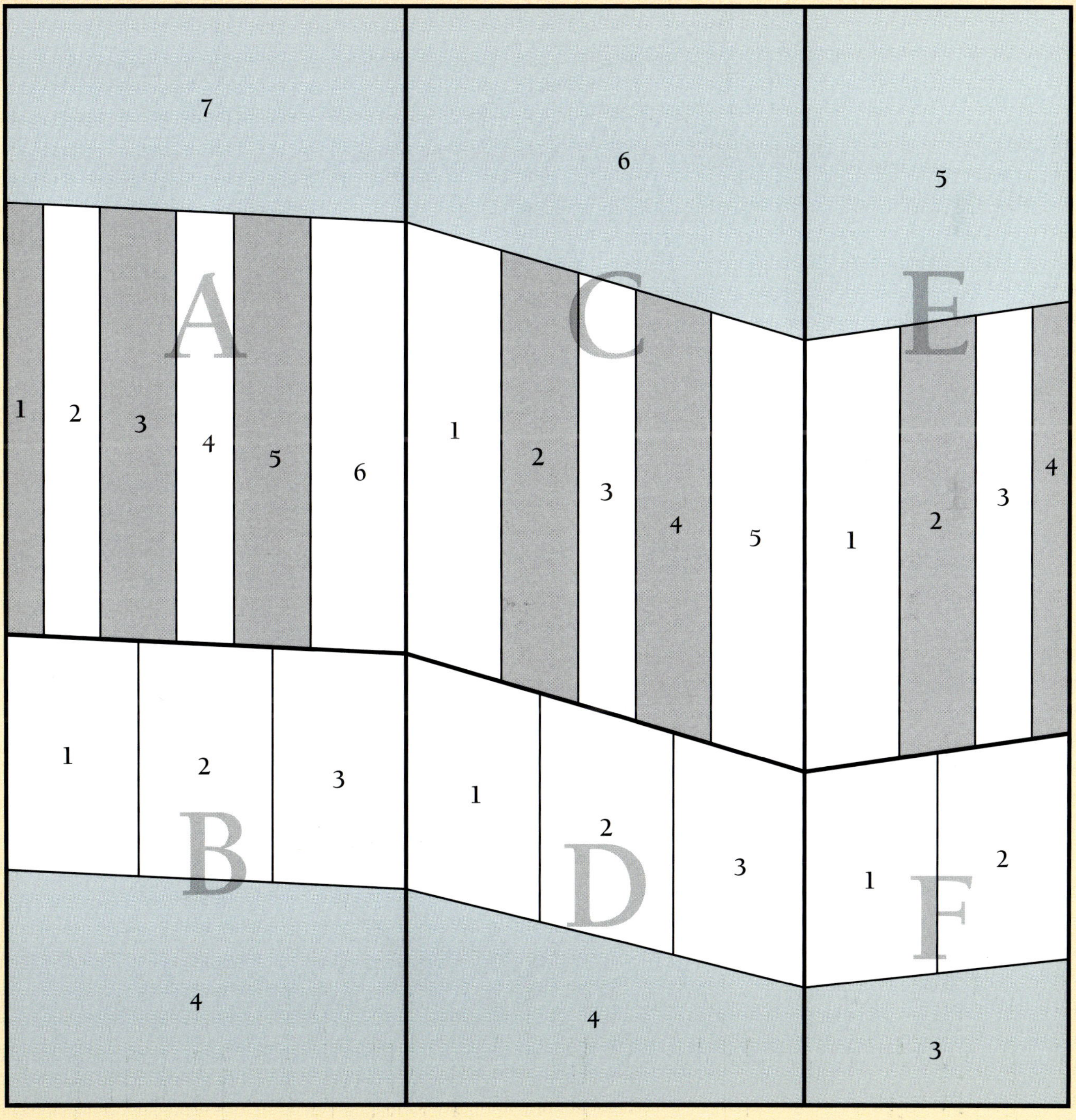

#4 Accordion

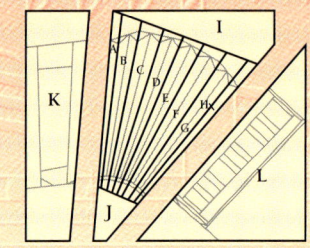

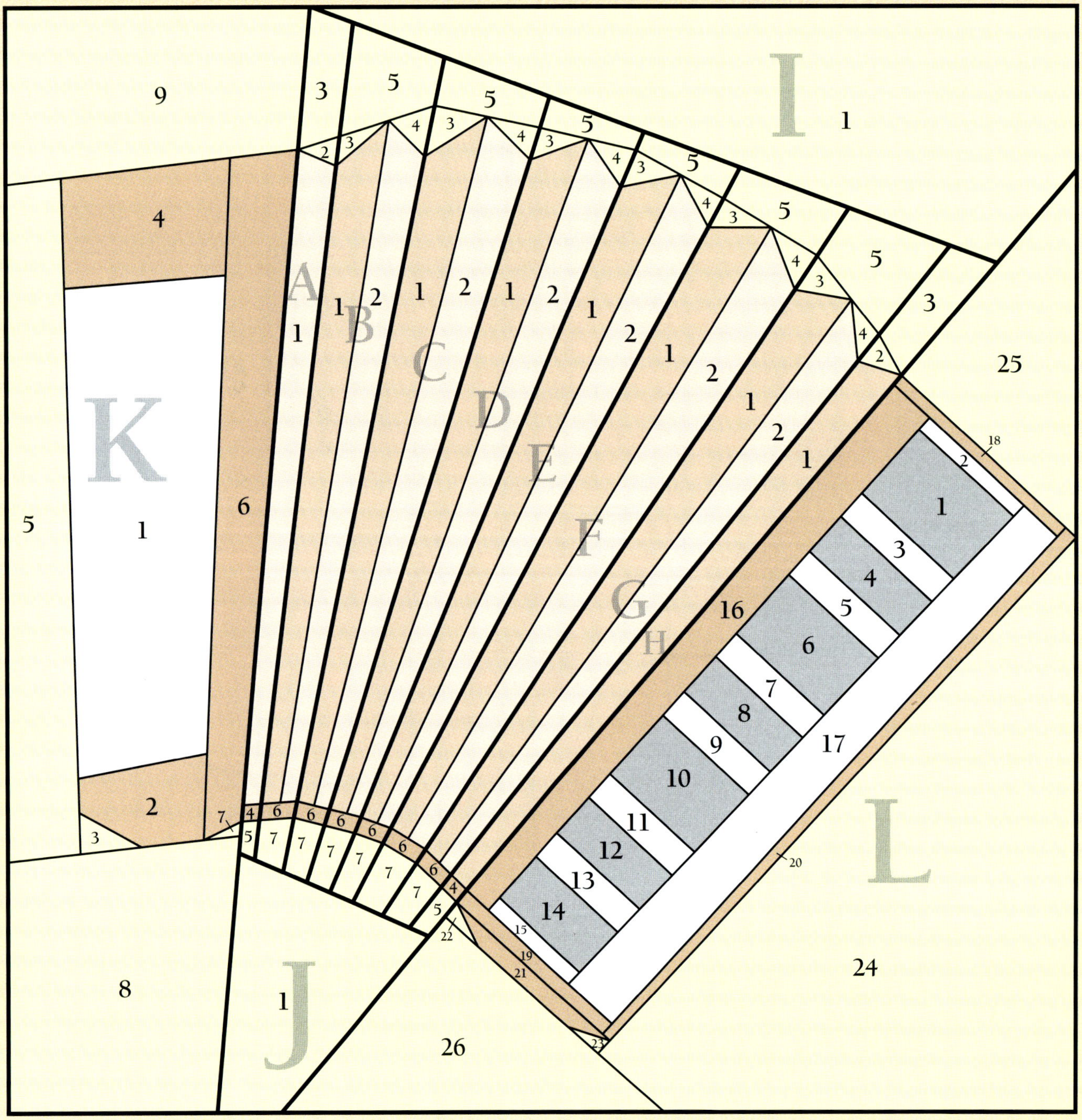

#5 Guitar

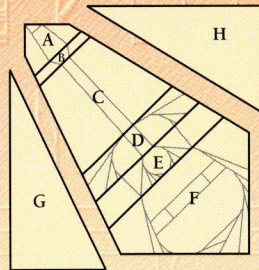

Special Notes:
Use one strand gray floss for guitar strings; couch with one strand gray floss. Straight stitch at base of strings with six strands gray floss. Attach six 5/8" wooden beads for pegs.

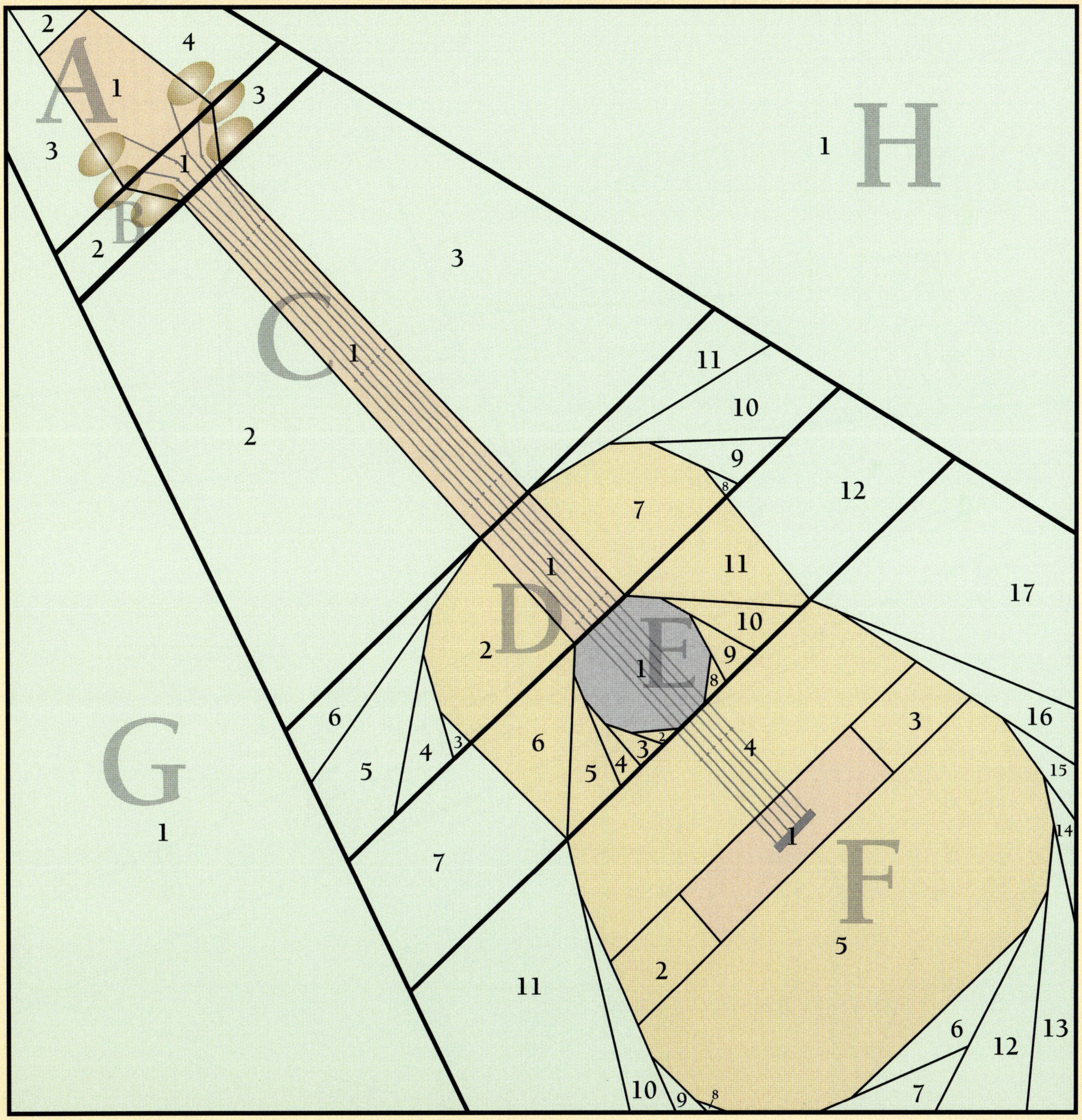

#6 Trombone

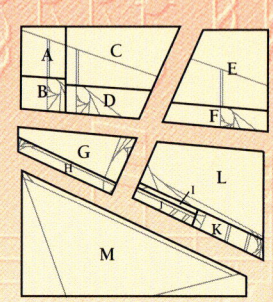

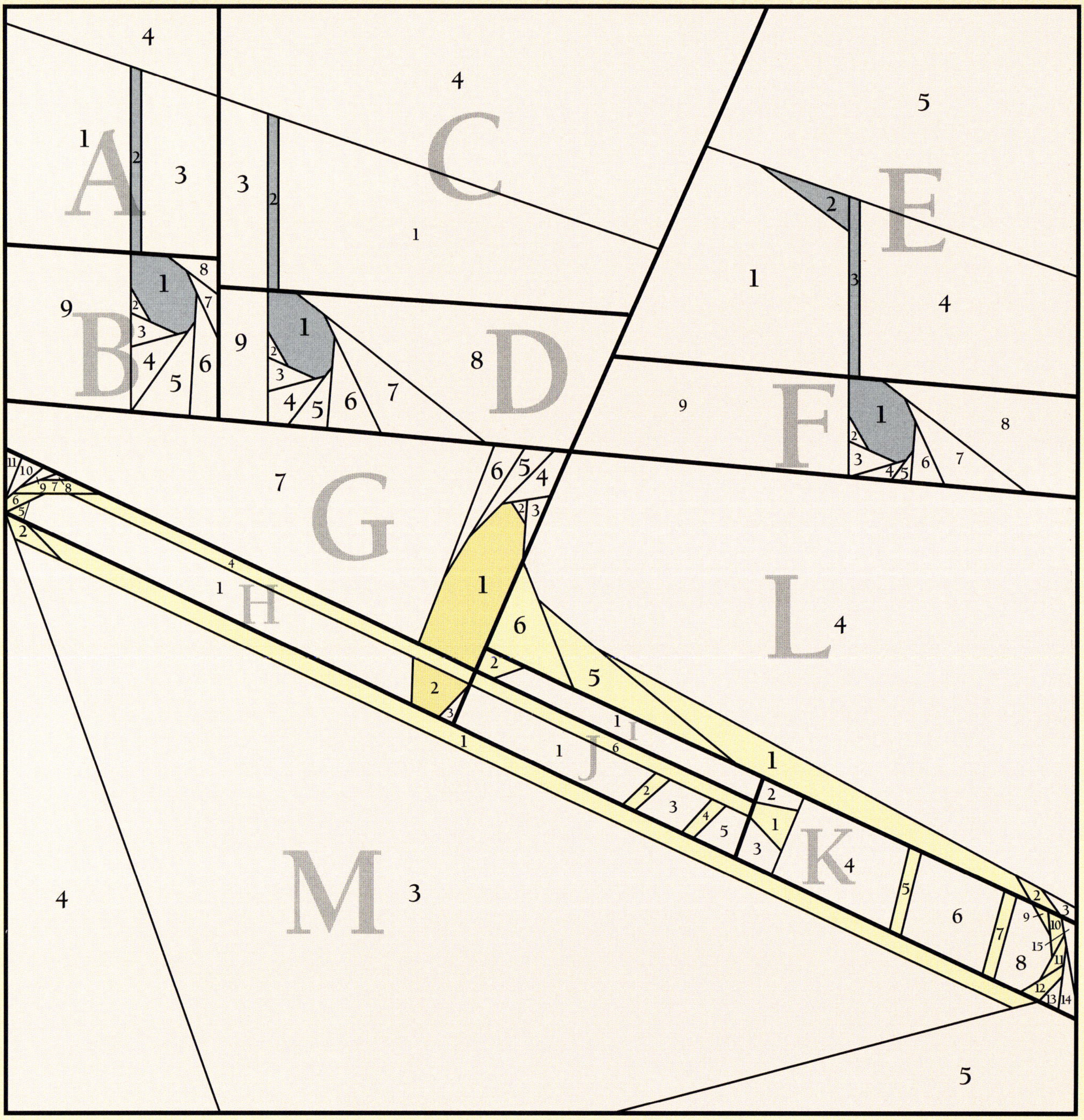

#7 Trumpet

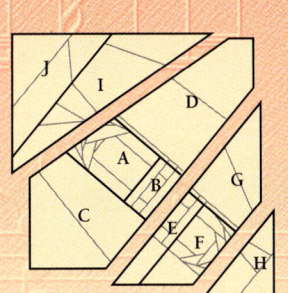

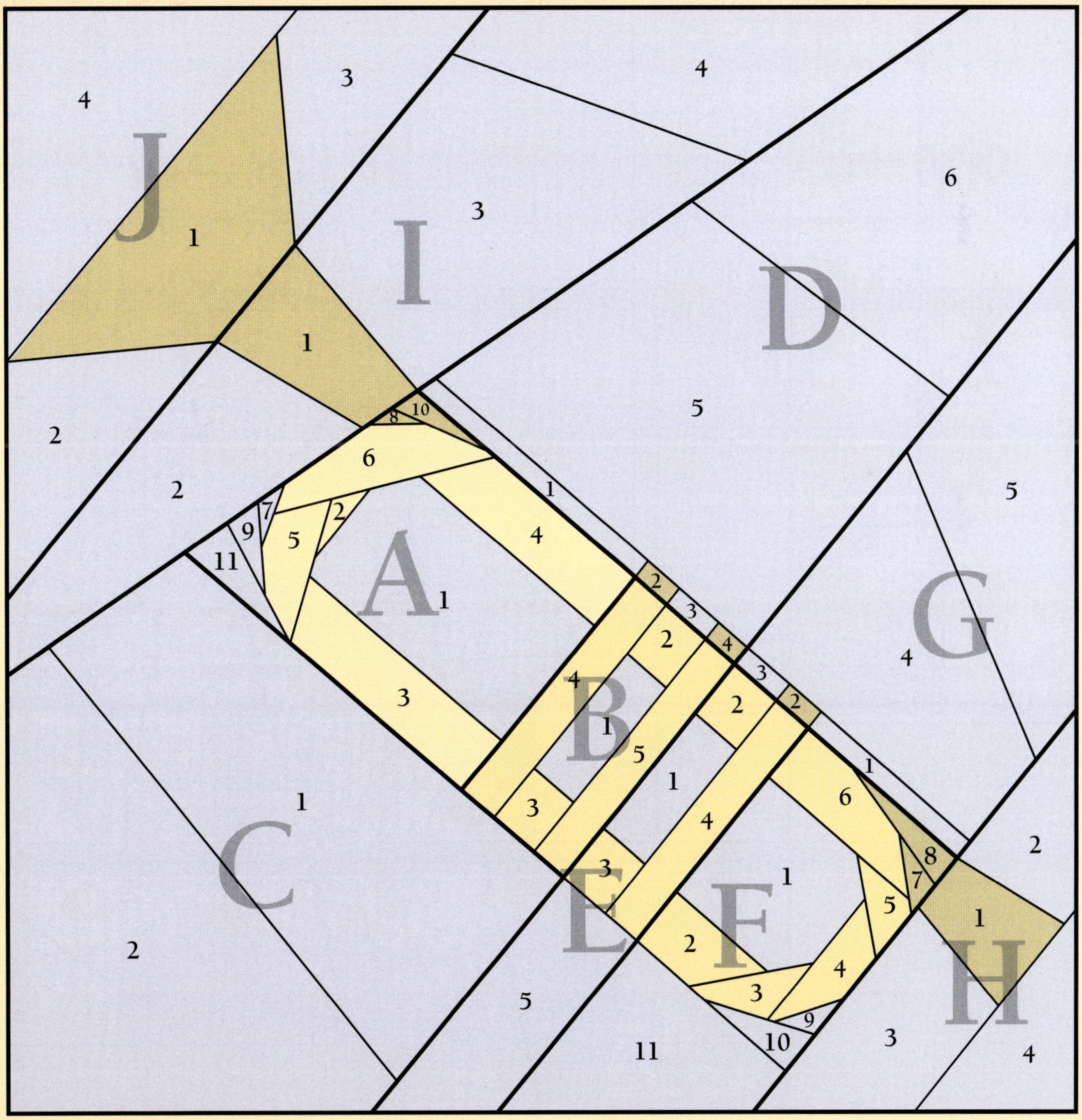

#8 Staff

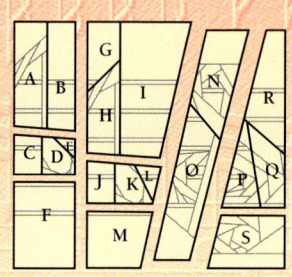

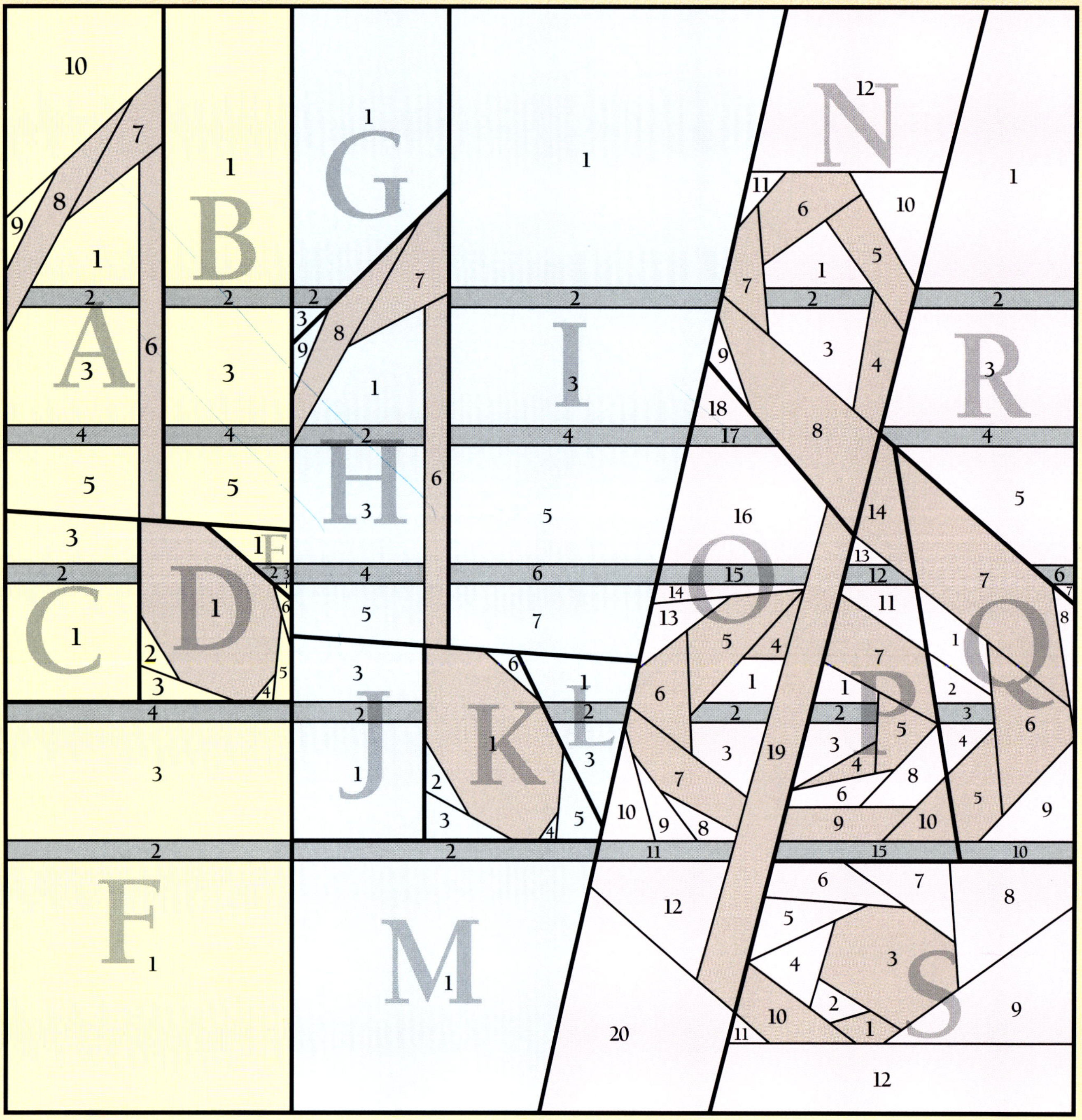

#9 Victrola

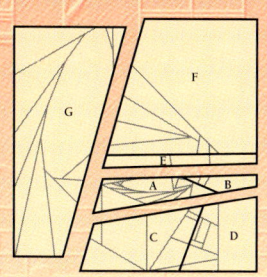

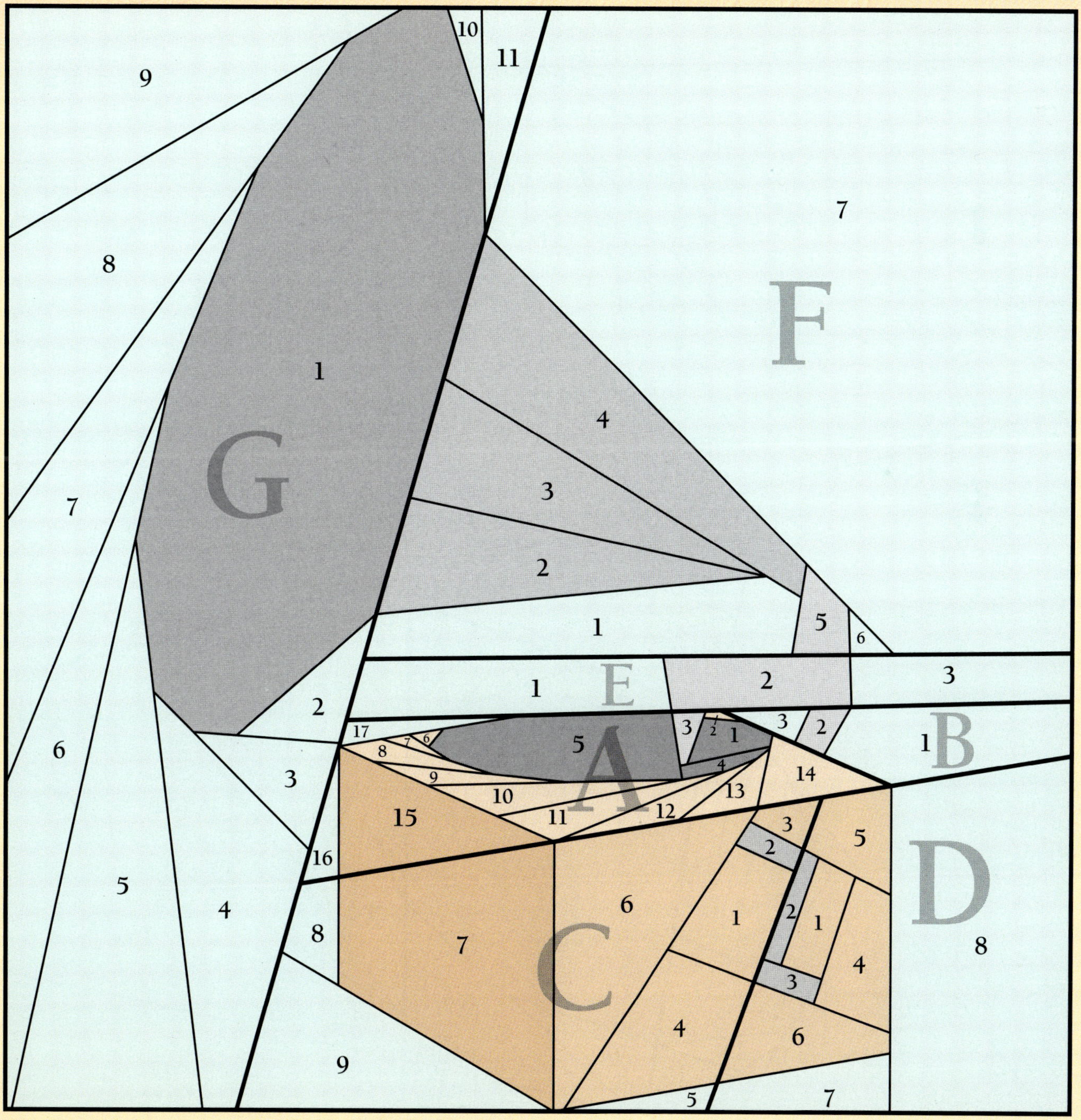

17

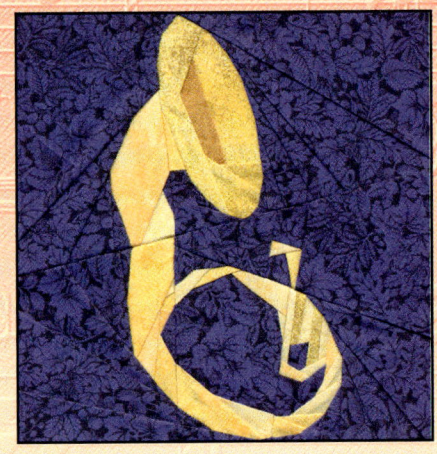

#10 Sousaphone

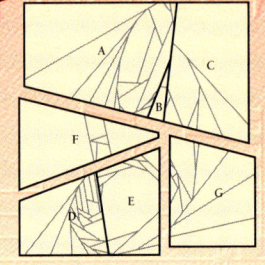

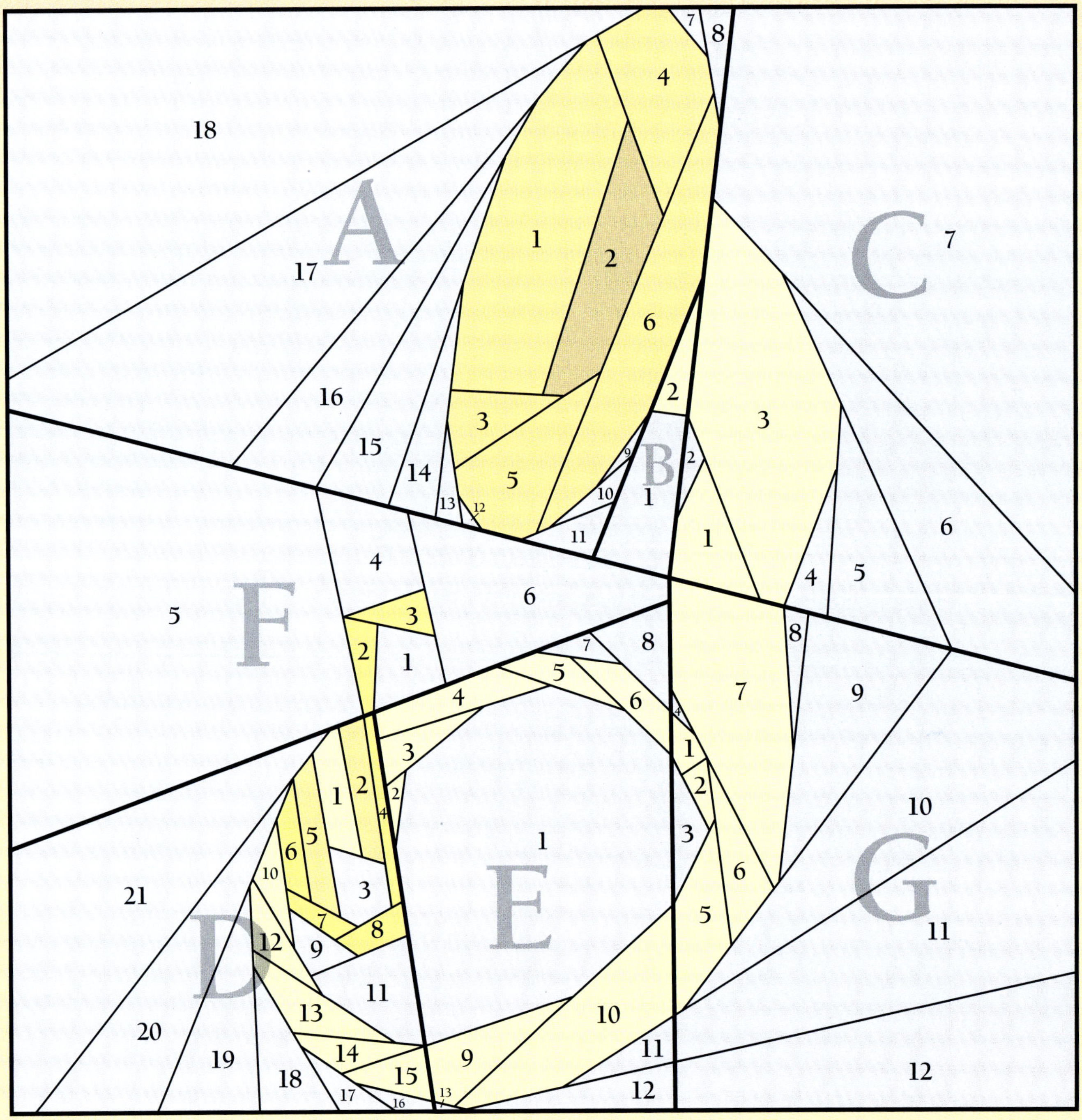

#11 Juke Box

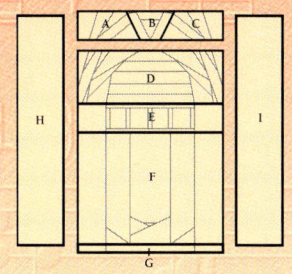

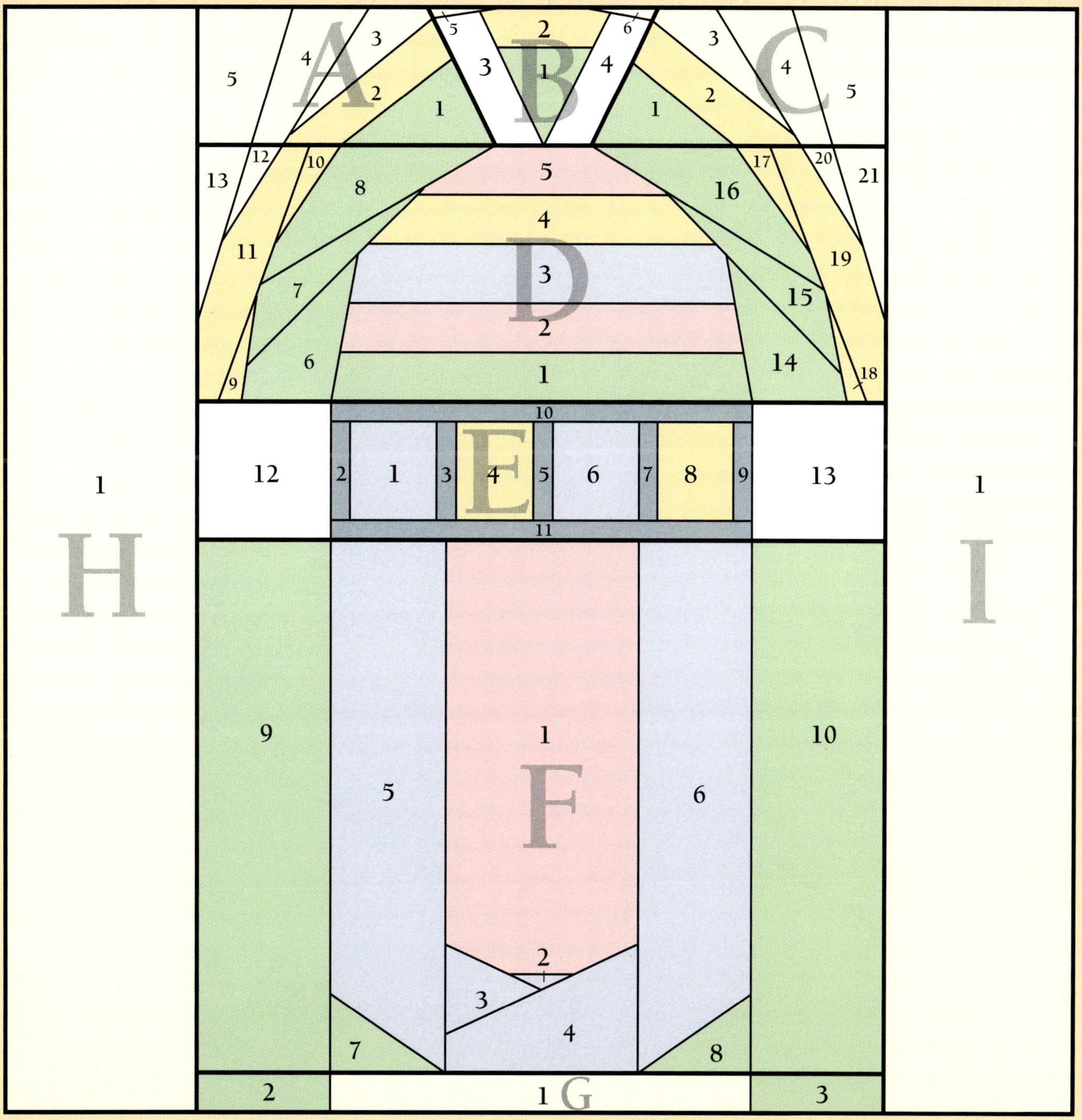

#12 Banjo

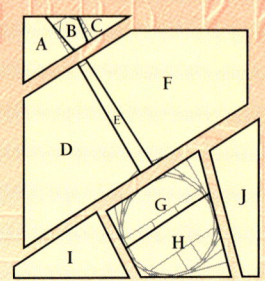

Special Notes:
Use one strand gray floss for banjo strings; couch with one strand gray floss.

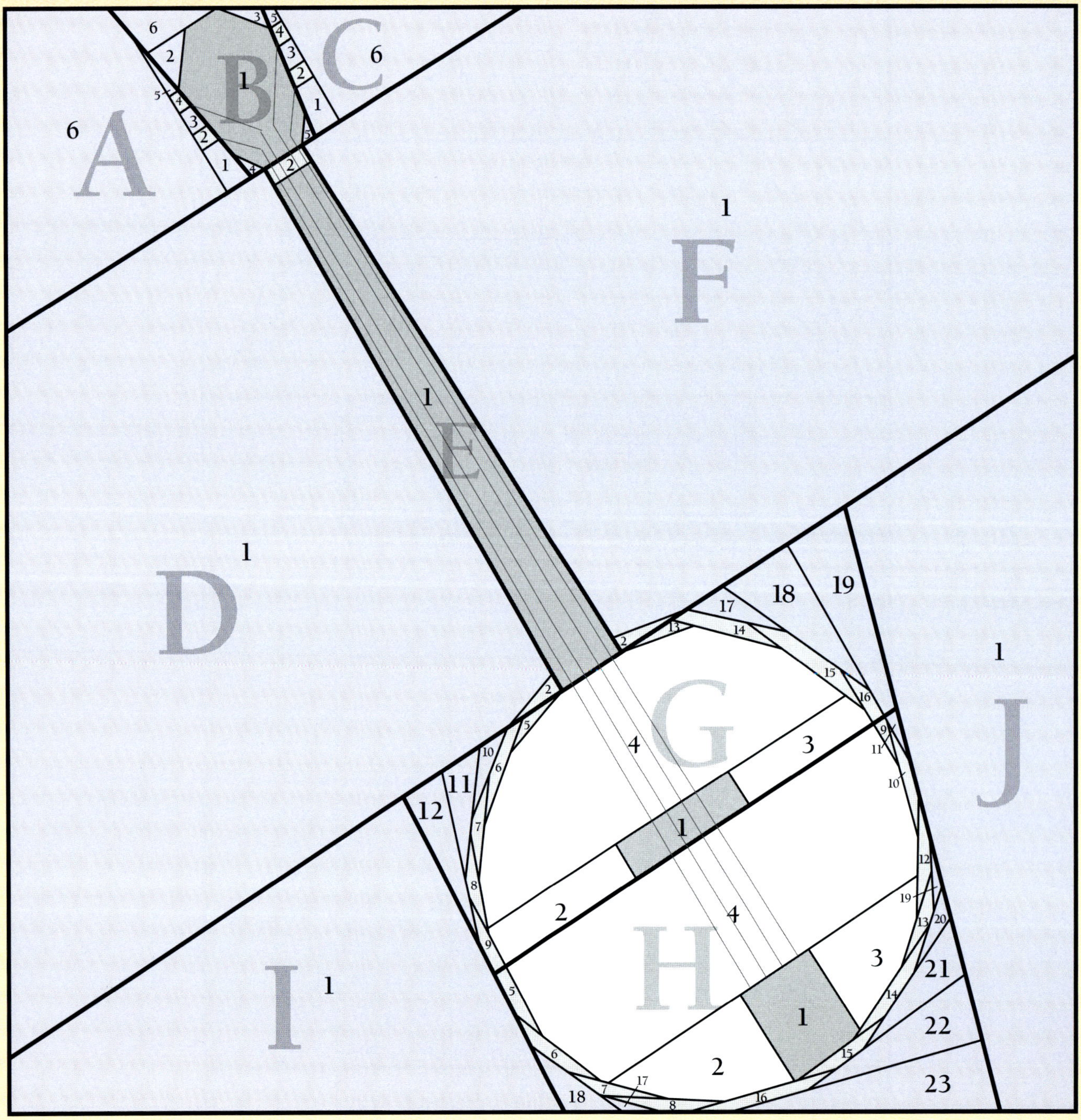

#13 Music Stand

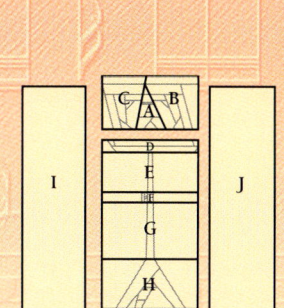

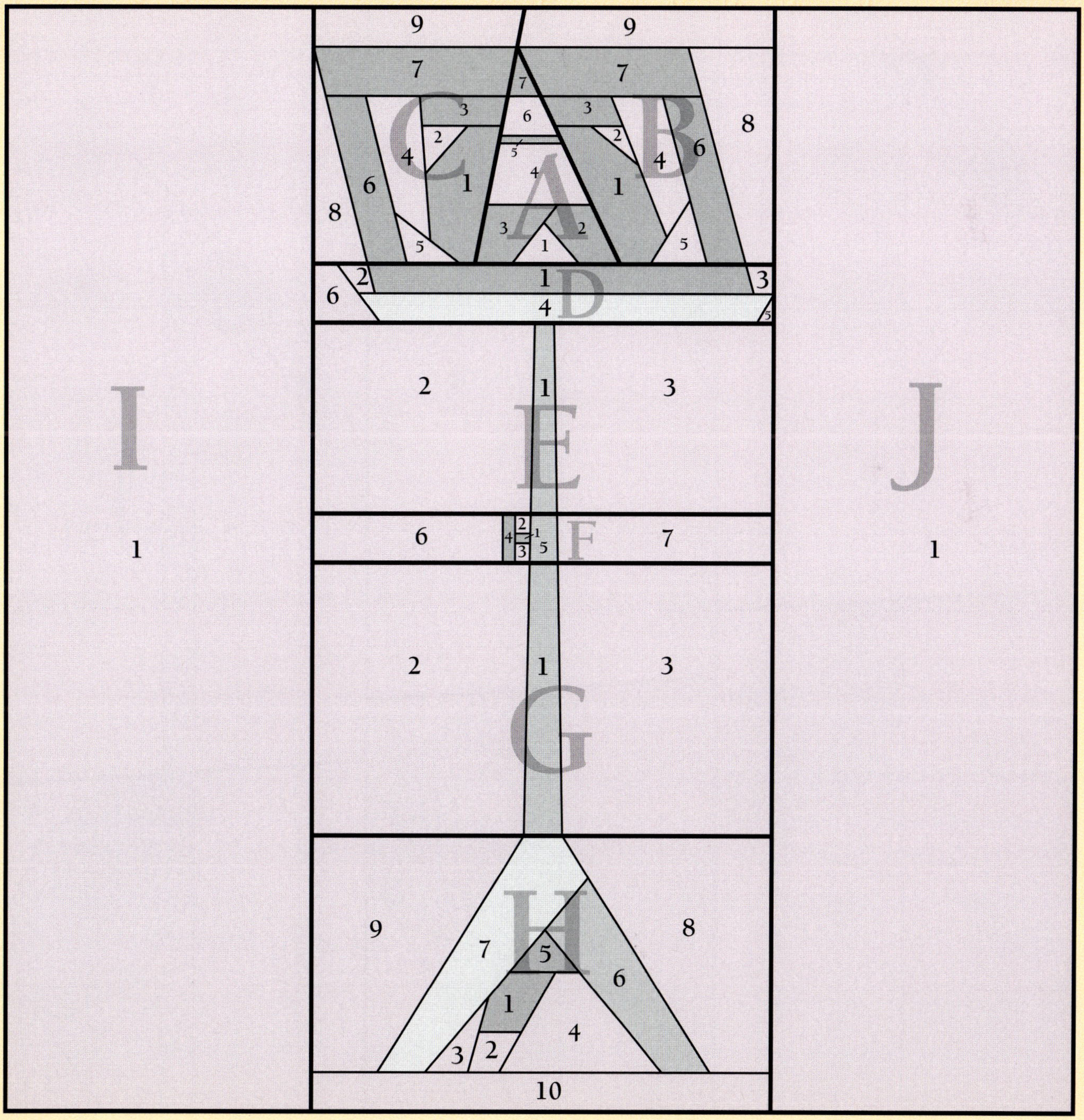

#14 Eighth Notes

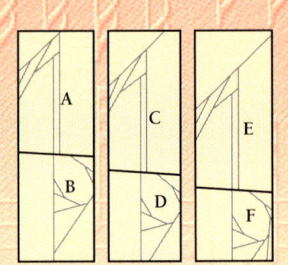

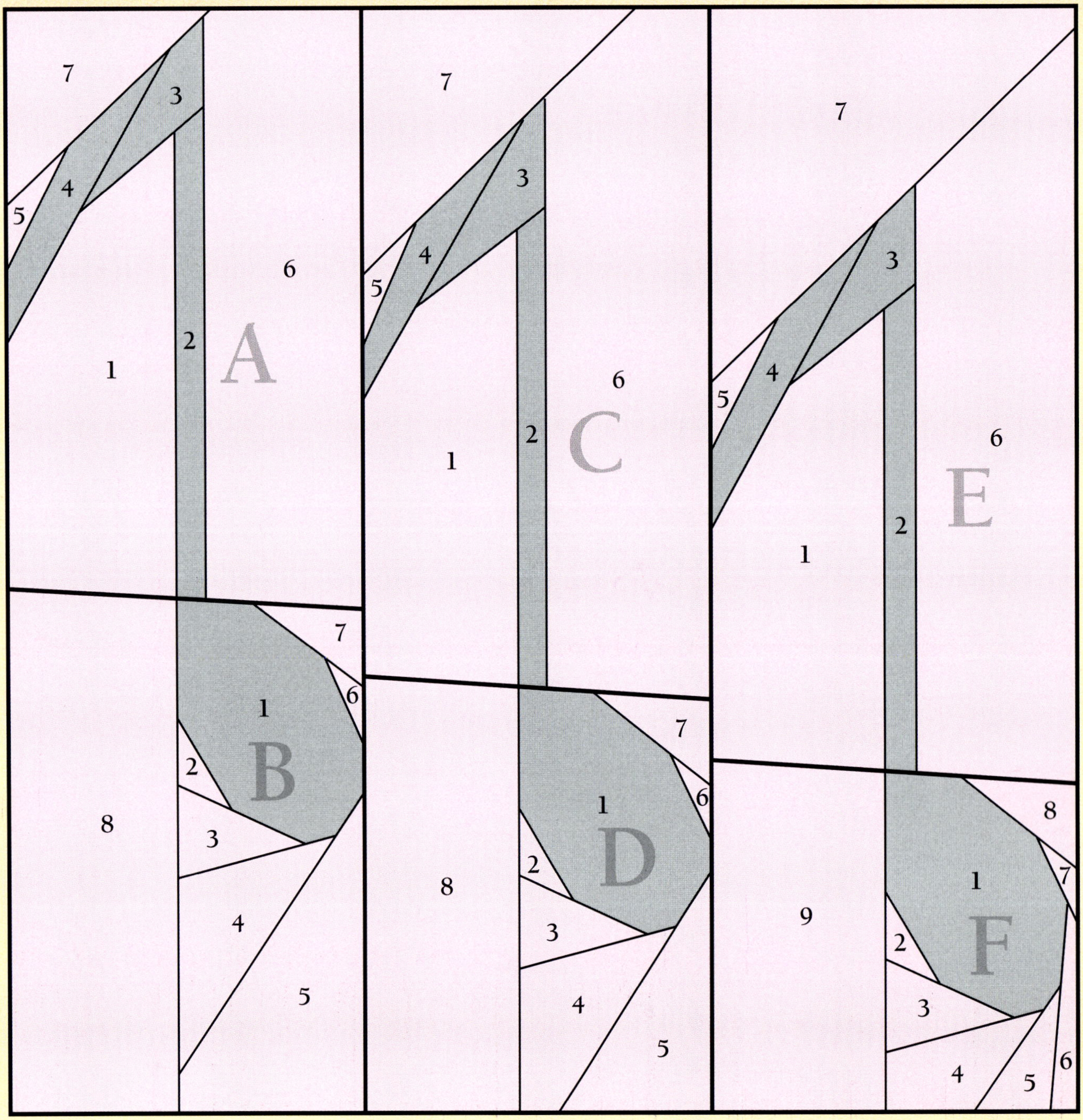

#15 Snare Drum

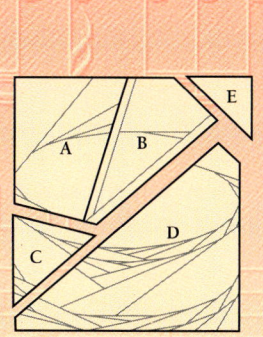

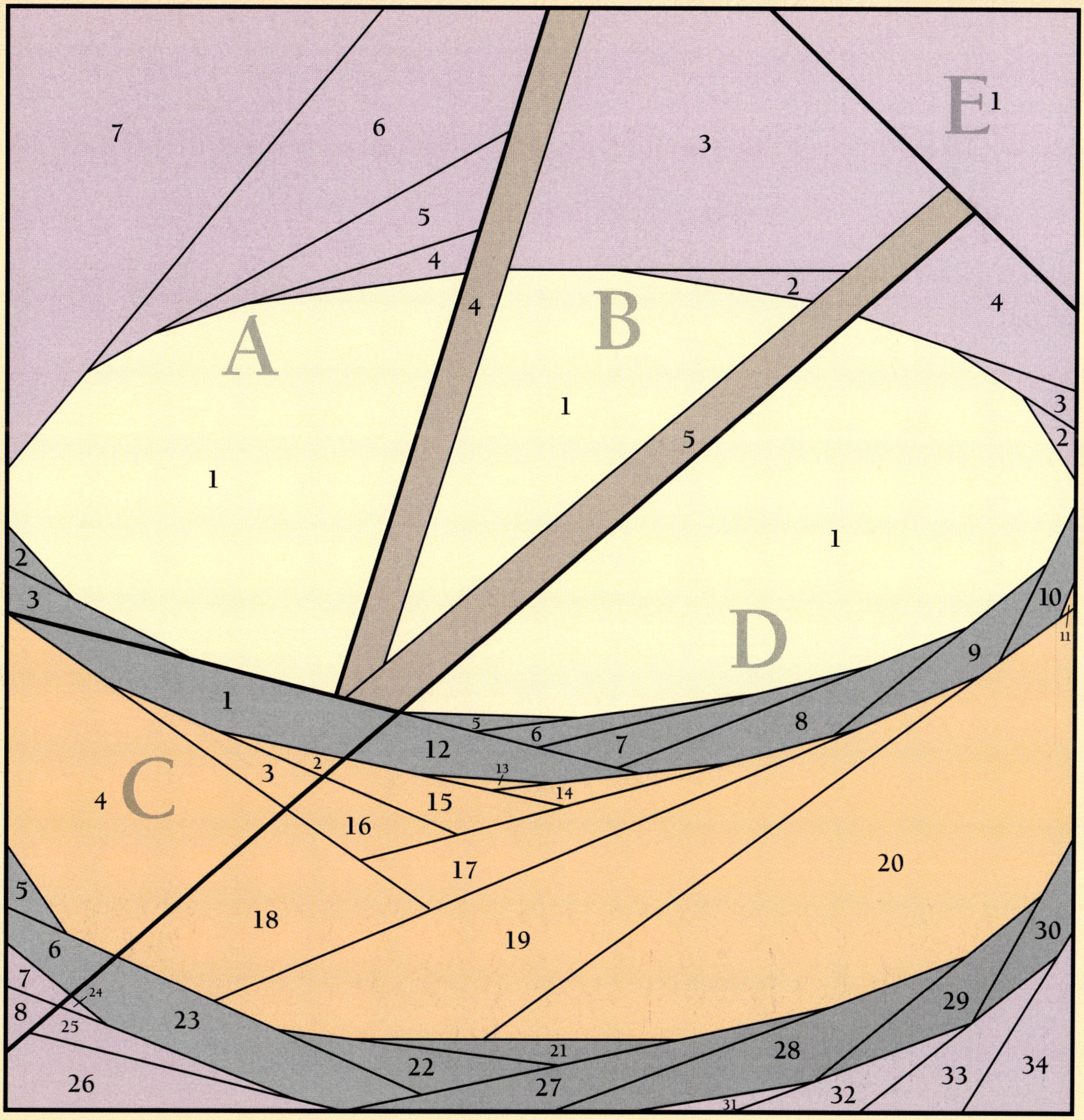

#16 Violin

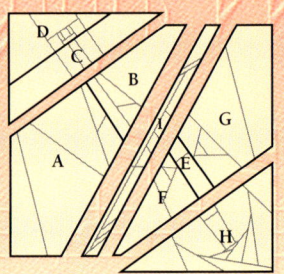

Special Notes:
Use one strand gray floss for violin strings; couch with one strand gray floss. Use three strands white floss for bow string; couch with one strand white floss. Attach four 5/8" wooden beads for pegs.

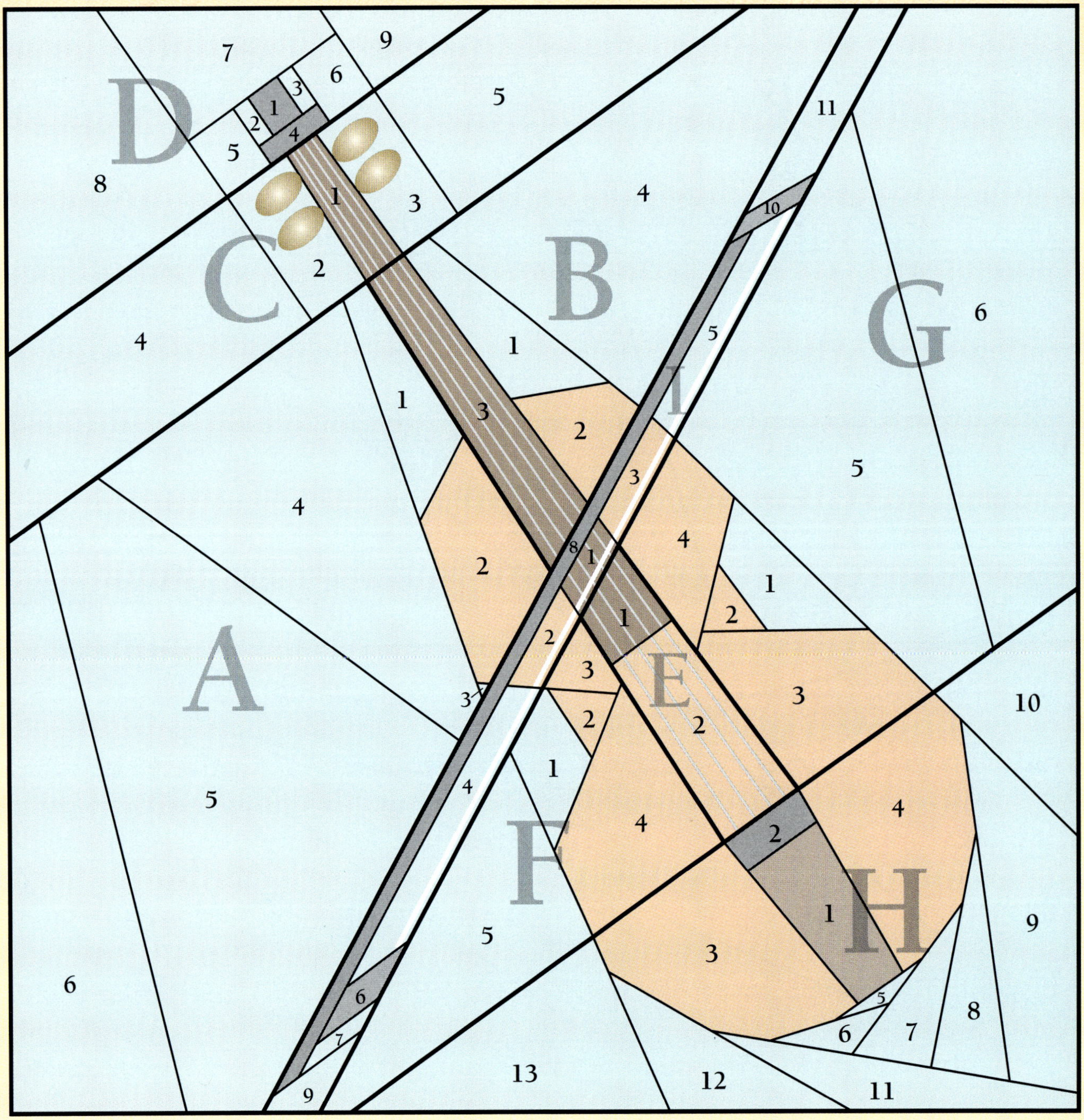

#17 Treble Clef

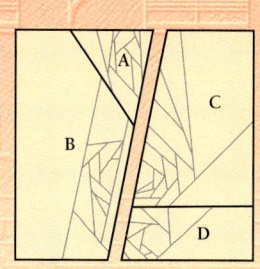

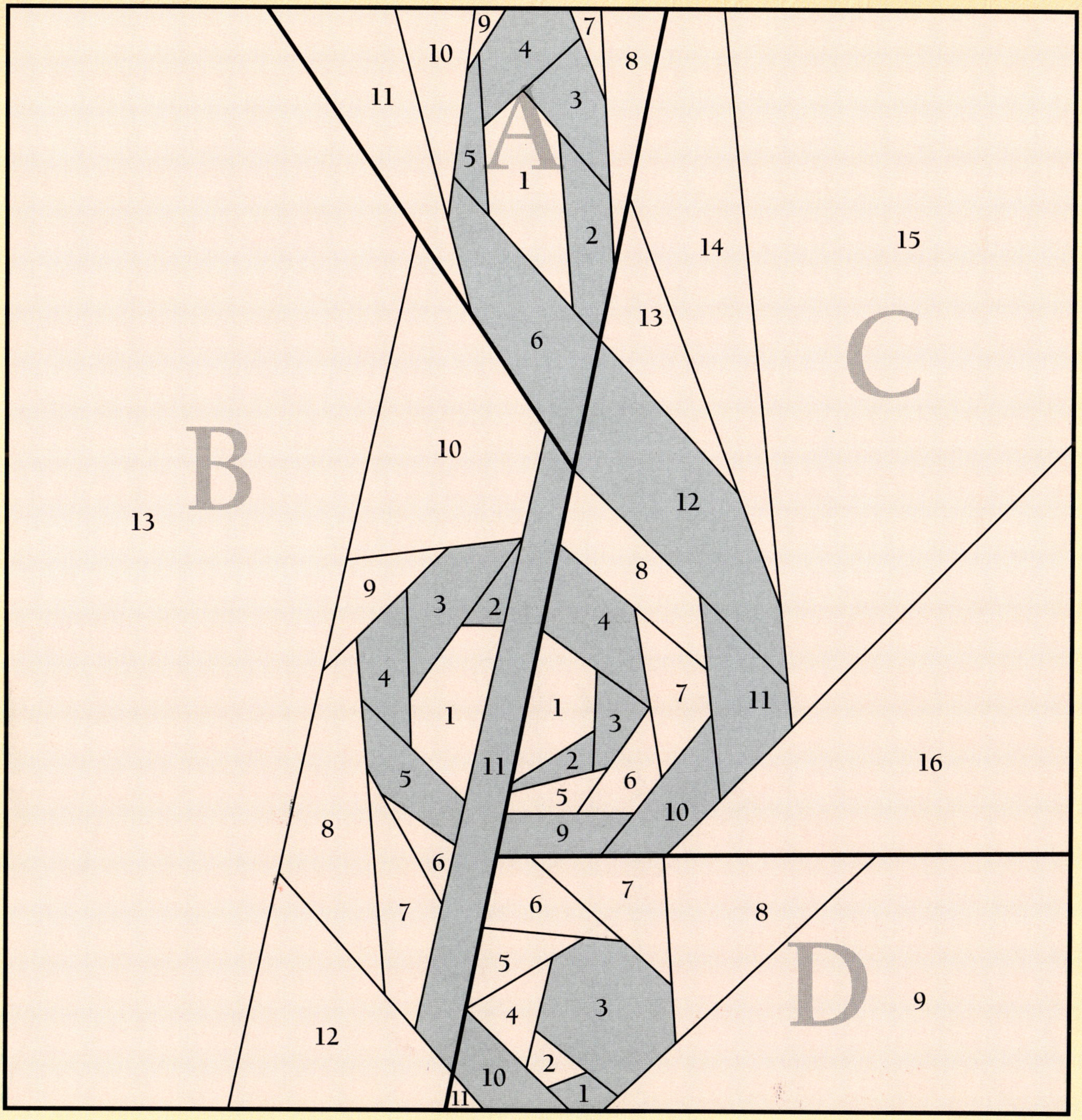

#18 Electric Guitar

Special Notes:
Use one strand gray floss for guitar strings; couch with one strand gray floss. Straight stitch with two strands black floss at top of each string. Attach four 1/4" silver ring beads and four black seed beads for pegs.

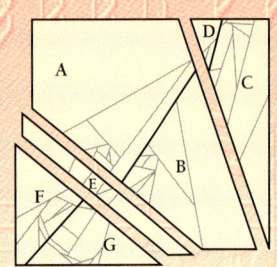

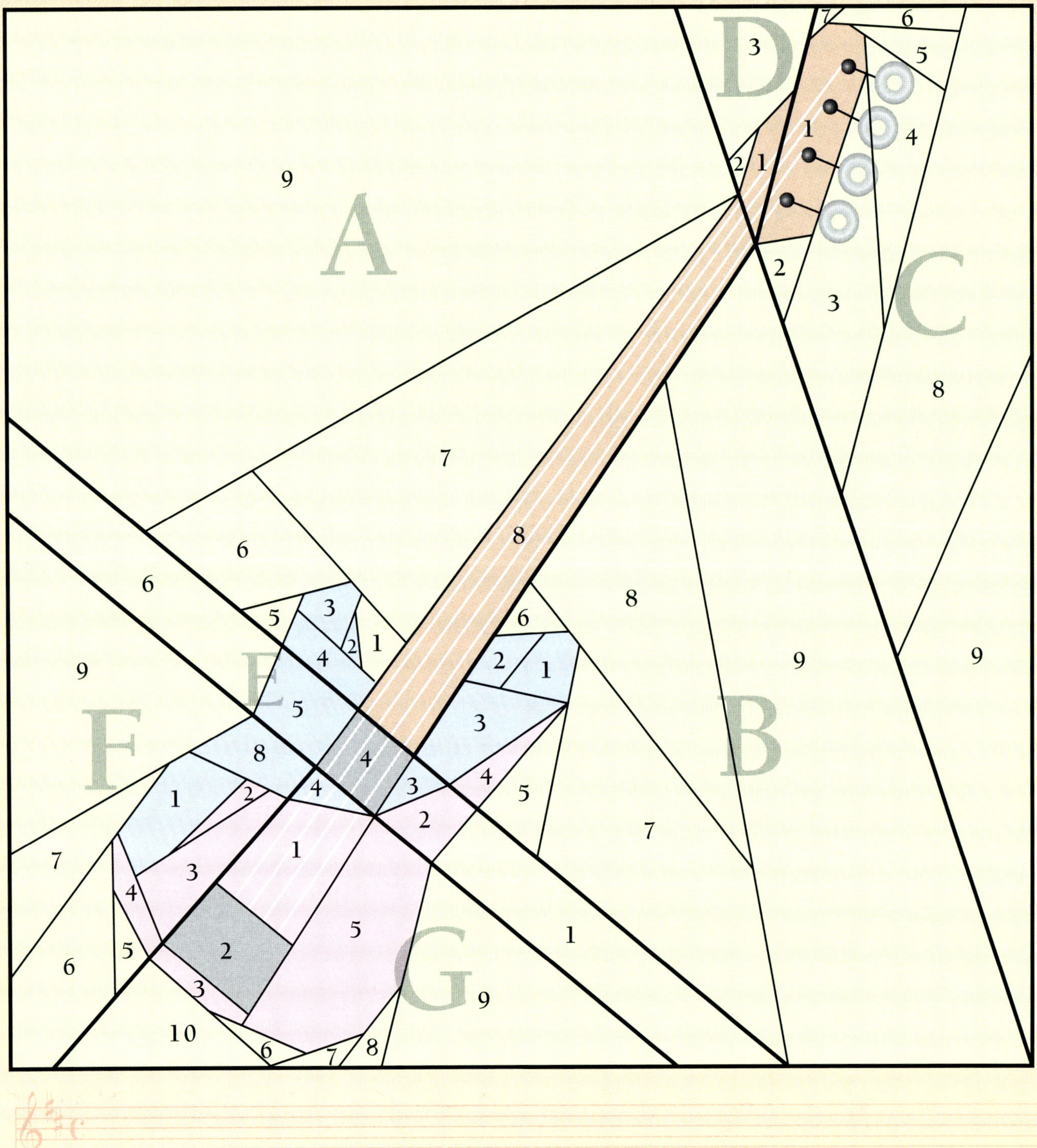

#19 Notes

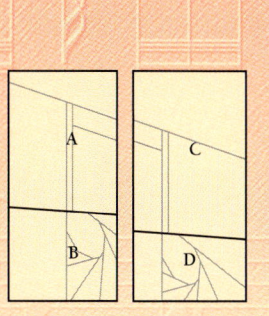

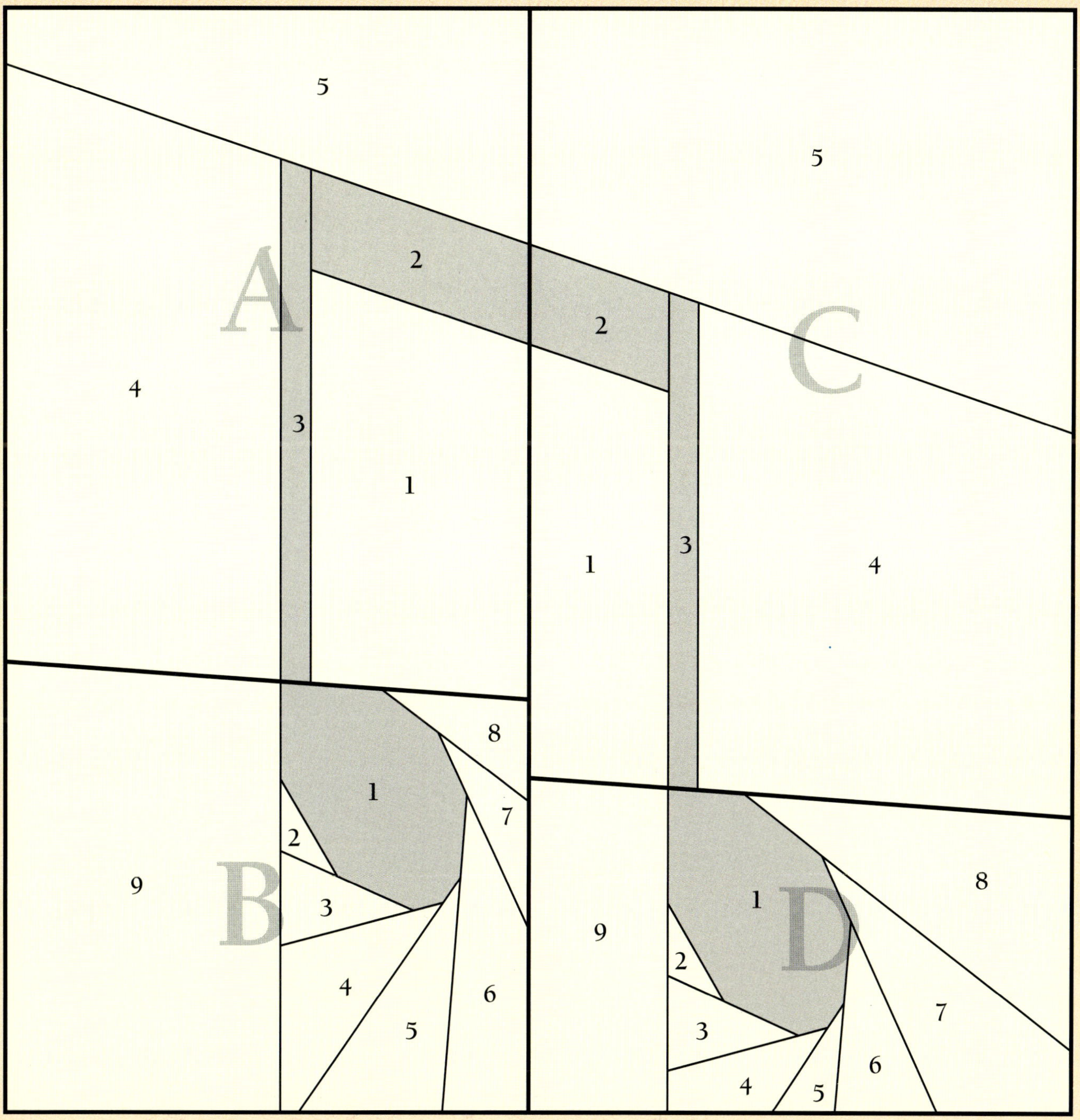

#20 Harp

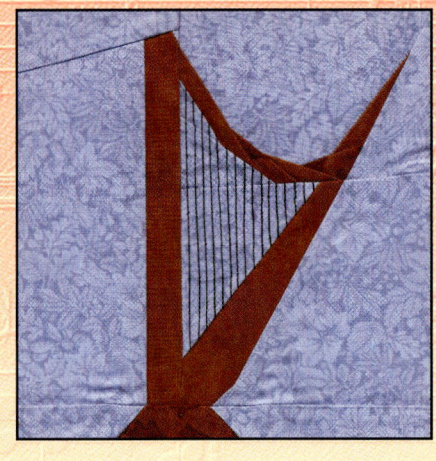

Special Note:
Use one strand black floss for harp strings; couch with one strand black floss.

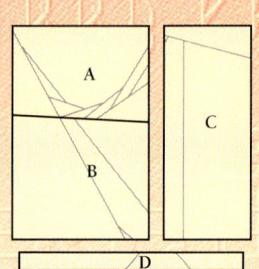

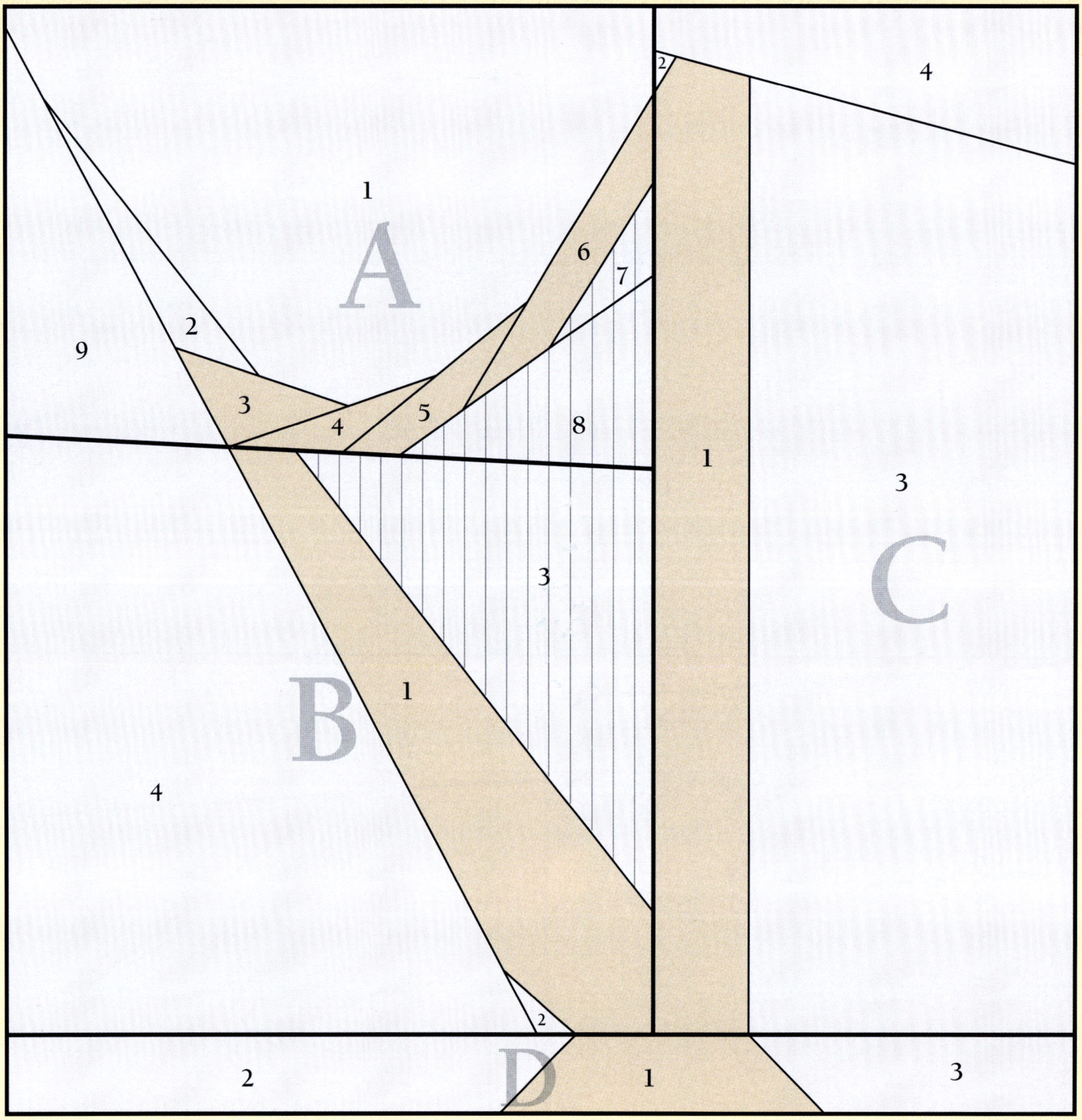

#21 Metronome

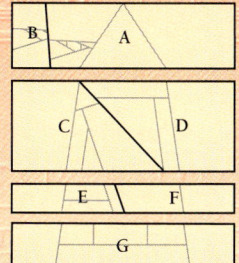

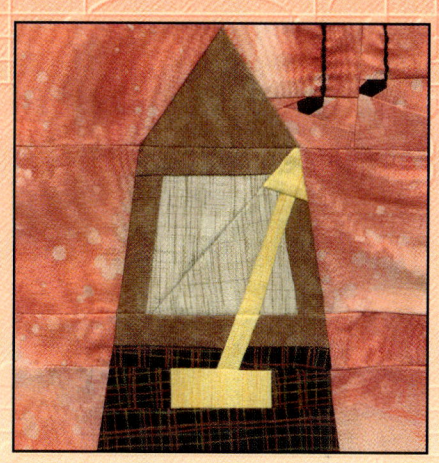

Special Note:
Backstitch note stems with six strands black floss.

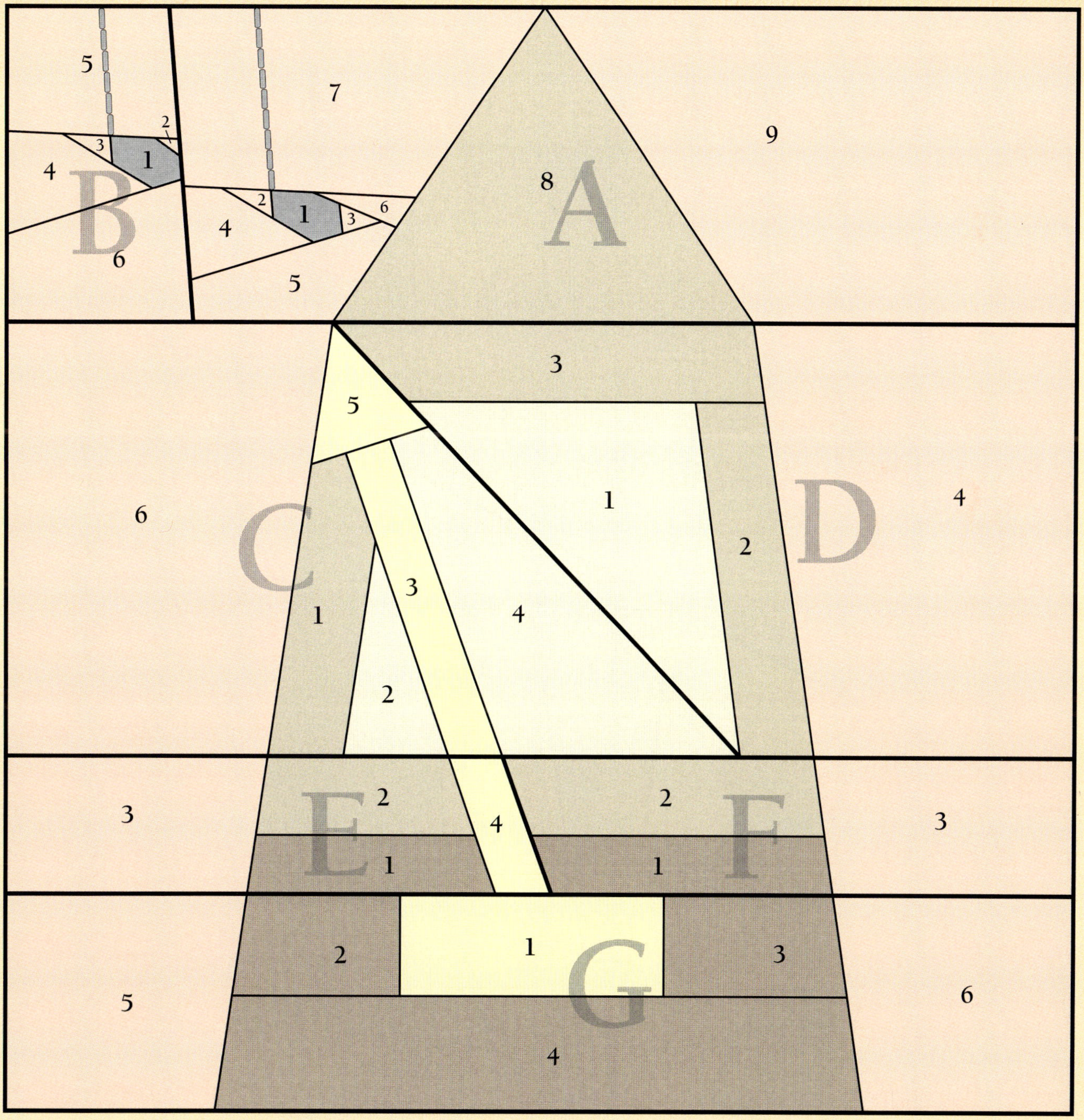

#22 Saxophone

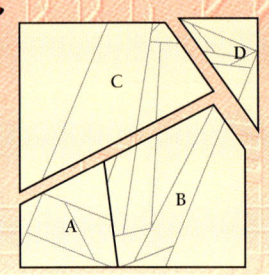

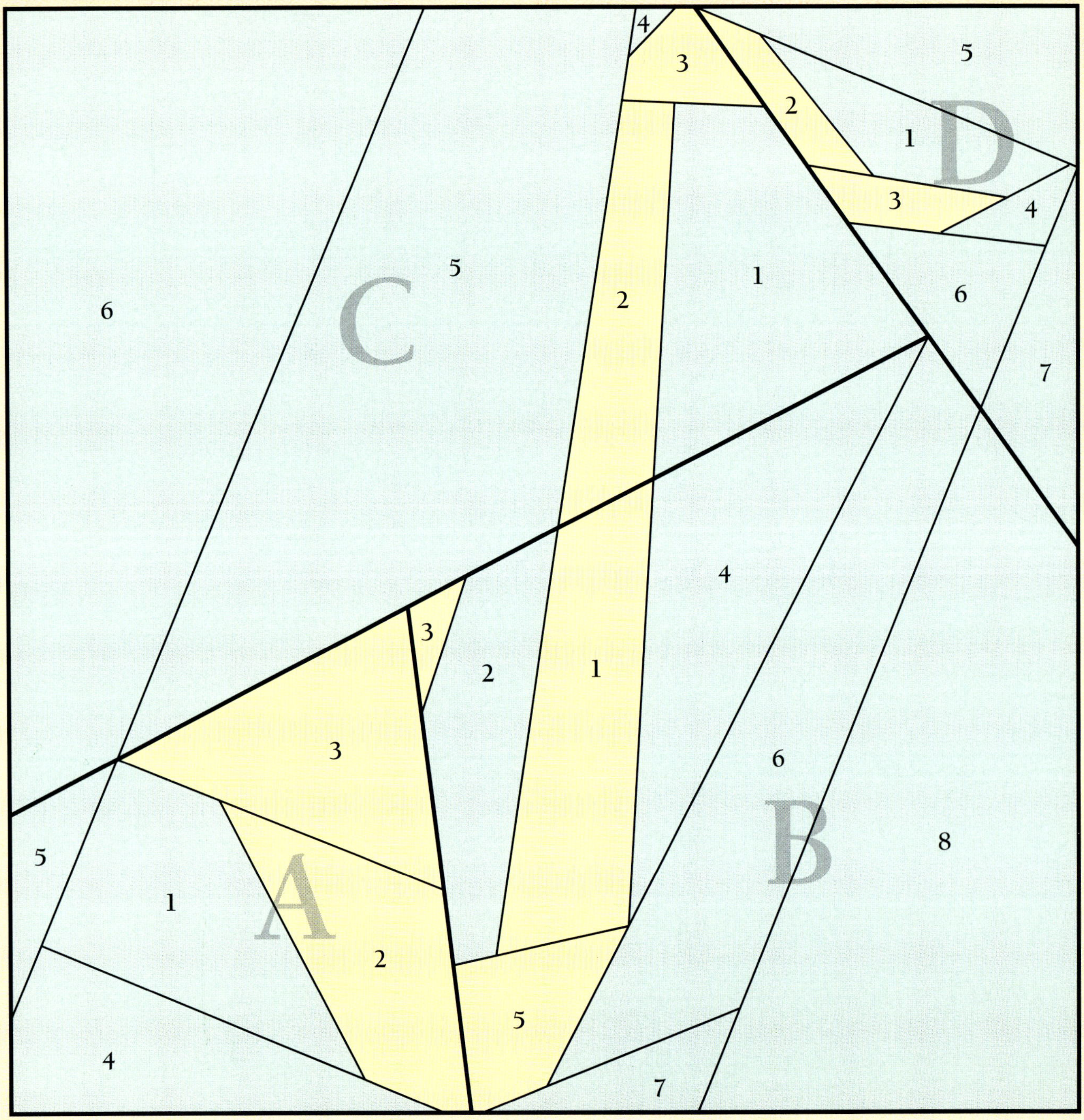

#23 Clarinet

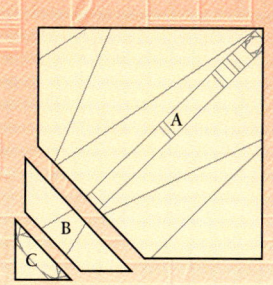

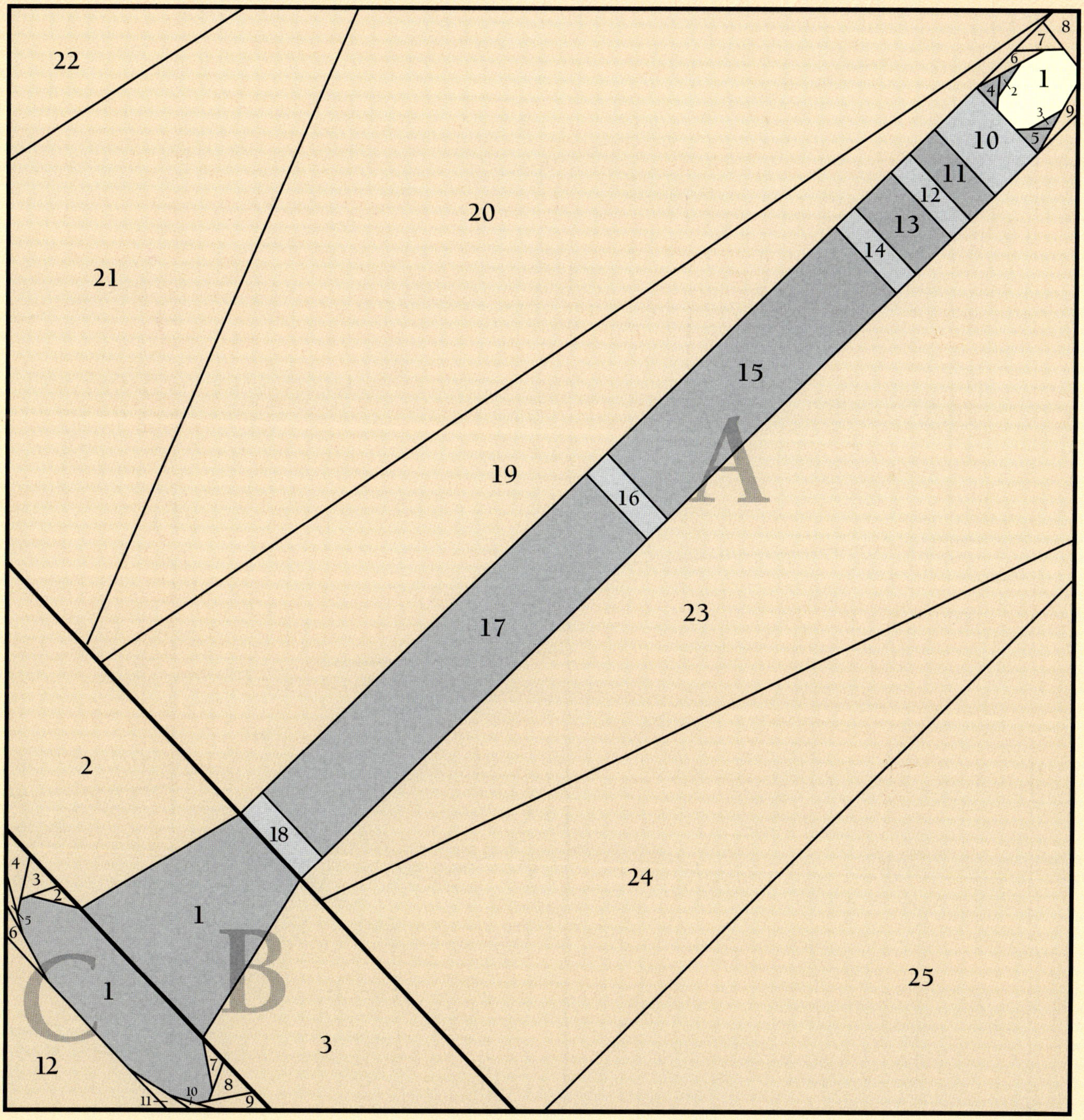

#24 Quarter Notes

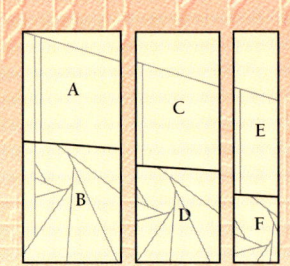

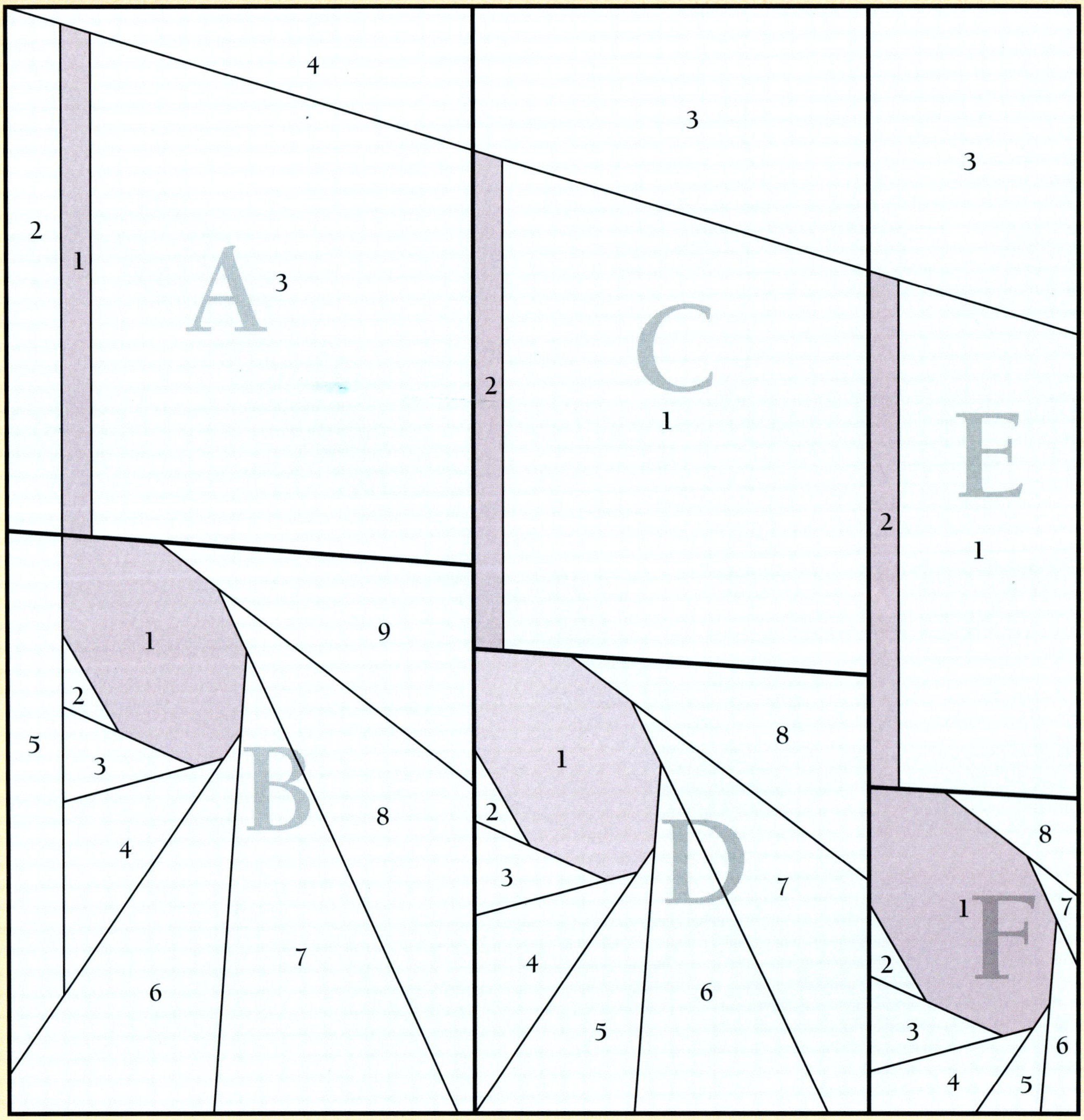